FIRE IN THE EUCALYPTS

A Wildland Firefighter's
Memoir of the
Black Saturday Bushfires

HAROLD R. LARSON

Tellwell Talent
www.tellwell.ca

ISBN

978-1-77302-363-2 (Hardcover)
978-1-77302-322-9 (Paperback)
978-1-77302-323-6 (eBook)

Contents

Introduction v

Prologue: The Pillars in the Distance. ix

Chapter 1:   Leaving Canada 1

Chapter 2:   Alexandra. 9

Chapter 3:   Camp Krusty 17

Chapter 4:   The Depot 27

Chapter 5:   Project Work. 35

Chapter 6:   Chrissy. 47

Chapter 7:   The Hunt. 55

Chapter 8:   One Tree Wonders 65

Chapter 9:   Beechworth Fire. 83

Chapter 10:   Black Saturday, February 7, 2009 93

Chapter 11:   Trapped in Marysville 105

Chapter 12:   The Aftermath 115

Chapter 13:   Rubicon. 123

Chapter 14:   The Grinding Blur 139

Chapter 15:   Relief. 149

Chapter 16:   She'll be Right Mate. 159

Introduction

Throughout my 17-year career as a Wildland Firefighter I have never, and hopefully never will again, experienced such a fire season as I did my first time in Australia during the Black Saturday bushfires. Even though I only spent less than half a year during that fire season in Alexandra, it has defined a huge part of my life. Some of my fondest memories along with some of my most difficult have come from that one Aussie summer.

After I returned home in the spring of 2009, I pushed the events that had transpired on Black Saturday to the back of my mind and locked them away. I removed myself from that life and from the friends that I came to care about. I felt that no one at home could relate to the loss and hardships that those people a world away had to endure, so I unknowingly let years pass until I began to accept what had happened. It was the ignorance of my younger self that truly kept me from learning from the most tragic of experiences, a type of learning that helps move the soul into a higher understanding of what it means to be human.

It was not until a couple of years had passed that I put my thoughts down on paper and started to comprehend the depth of my experience and how important it would be to share my story. With help from a journal that I had kept and pictures that I had taken during my time in Alexandra, I began to piece this memoir together. However, when writing I found that there was still a lot of that summer that I didn't understand and couldn't piece together in my mind. Over time some memories remained as clear as if they had happened yesterday, while others had become foggy and full of gaps.

It wasn't until five years later when I returned to Alexandra for another season as a wildland firefighter that I was able to complete this story. Being back in the area where it had all taken place and talking to my friends and co-workers about their experiences during that fire season made this story easier to write.

It was clear that the loss was still felt in the community, and even after all those years, some of my friends did not like to talk about those fires. I changed the names of select people out of respect for those who might not want to be a part of this story or who might find it easier to leave that part of their life in the past.

It is strange how stress and extraordinary circumstances can shape a person's memory. One of the Aussie firefighters told me that six months after the 2009 fire season, he held individual debriefs with all of the firefighters who had been in Marysville on Black Saturday. He said it was surprising how everyone had a slightly different version about the events that had happened and the timeline on which they had occurred. I have written this record to the best of my recollection and tried my utmost to capture my experiences without bias.

The bravery of these men and women should be commended. They fought through their fears and displayed great selflessness in knowingly putting themselves in danger to protect what they hold close to their hearts. I am grateful for the opportunity to have seen the resilience of the human spirit and to witness what a community can endure if they work together.

The Pillars in the Distance

Lying in my bed soaked from the pool of my own sweat, I scanned the walls and ceilings for any huntsman spiders that could be lurking around looking for a snack. Throughout the summer, these spiders the size of my hand had constantly invaded my house and patrolled the walls of my bedroom searching for insects to feed on. After my standoff with the first one that had come crawling into my room several months earlier, I had decided it was best for me to just leave them alone and let them continue in their hunts for the other crawly things taking up residence in my house. The spiders and I had come to the mutual understanding that if I left them alone, they would repay me in kind.

Water was the first thought on my mind after making sure I was safe from the giant spiders. Throwing on a pair of black shorts that I had brought from back home, I walked from my bedroom into the kitchen. I opened the fridge and poured myself a large glass of cold water that I chugged down almost as fast as it was poured to help stay ahead of the constant battle for hydration. Feeling slightly refreshed, I poured myself another glass and walked outside onto the grey wooden porch to see what the day might have in store for me.

Even at this early hour, as soon as I stepped out from the protection of my house I could feel my skin instantly start to burn from the lack of ozone between me and the ever-shining sun. Without a cloud in the sky, the relentless beating down of solar rays made it hard to accomplish anything in the direct sunlight. A bluish tint was visible in the air caused by the massive amount of oil evaporating out of the eucalyptus leaves. The temperature was already in the low–30s, and with no relief in sight, today promised to be another cooker of a day. The Canadian in me was wondering how people could live like this.

From the weathered porch, I could see my not-so-favourite feathered alarm clocks hanging awkwardly from branches, eating fruit, and talking to each other. I used to imagine that living in an area with exotic birds would be a treat; however, the magic soon disappeared after being woken up at every daybreak to the exasperating calls of the cockatoos. The throaty, choking sounds that struggled to come from each of these white birds with yellow mohawks had nothing majestic about them. Several cockatoos from the cemetery across the street flew clumsily over to join their neighbours for breakfast in my backyard. Their ungraceful struggle to keep in the air seemed to perfectly match their irritating calls to one another.

Looking at the dull green and brown hills that surrounded the town, I could see that the landscape was as dry as ever. This area was experiencing an eight-year drought which had a direct impact on the local flora and fauna. Creeks, waterholes, and sloughs that had been prevalent only a decade earlier were now a rare sight. Their absence was causing stress on anything that needed any amount of water to survive, including the people who lived there.

For the second consecutive weekend I had been asked to be on-call, ready to race to the Fire Depot at a moment's notice in case any fires broke out in the area. For the last two-and-a-half months I had been working five days a week as a Wildland Firefighter for the Department of Sustainability and Environment. Now that the fire hazard was extreme, I would have to be ready at all times to be dispatched to a wildfire.

Though I had fought a couple of small fires in the previous weeks, I wasn't too concerned about anything starting today. I was more absorbed by the challenge of how to stay cool in this country where the sun and the heat always seemed to be winning. Looking at the clear blue sky and not seeing any cumulous clouds that could throw out lightning and potentially start new fires, I retreated into the shelter of my single-storey house. In my naivety, I fell into a false sense of security that there was not much chance of any fires starting today, rational-izing that a forest fire would start here the same way as it did in my home district on the other side of the world - largely by lightning.

Both of my roommates were gone for the weekend, so I had the house to myself. I moved across the polished hardwood floors in the living room and turned on the morning news. The weatherman from Melbourne with his quick Aussie accent went on to describe that the temperatures would be well above 40°C for the third consecutive day and to stay out of the sun as much as possible. As if anyone needed that advice after being assaulted by this heat wave over the last couple of days.

In my non-air-conditioned house, just sitting on the couch required more effort than it should have. The two portable fans in the living room that blew stale warm air in my direction did little to cool me down. The only relief seemed to be when I would submerge myself in cold water. Since the cool water running out of Lake Eildon into the Goulburn River was farther away than I was willing to walk, a cold shower would have to suffice. I had to be conscious not to stay in the shower for too long with respect to the town's water usage policy. The people of the State of Victoria had had to adapt to their new circumstances of drought and change some of their practices to handle the dry conditions they were now facing. One solution to help mitigate this problem was to limit everyone to four-minute showers. I am not sure how they came up with this magic number, but it was a standard rule in place that everyone took seriously. Stuck onto the inside of our shower wall was a small hourglass filled with blue sand that when turned would fill the other end in exactly four minutes. Before having to adhere to this rule, I had taken for granted the endless supply of fresh water there is in Canada. Here, the cold water always helped, but only for a short time. I would have to keep my showers brief if I wanted to stay under the four-minute rule.

Continually sipping on water, I lay down on the old brown couch and surfed through the only five channels that were available. Of course cricket was on. This game was as much a staple here as the beer. A cricket test-match could last up to five days and provide a distraction over the dog days of summer. Over the last two months I had come to enjoy watching this foreign sport where 11 men on two teams competed on a round grass field for cricket superiority. This game where a man would bowl a hard red ball at speeds over 100km/hr aimed at wickets behind a batter was a beloved national pastime for the majority of Australians.

As I lay on the couch slipping in and out of consciousness, the morning turned into afternoon. During breaks in the cricket match, weather updates constantly reinforced how hot it was. Thank you, weatherman, for filling me in on what everyone is the State of Victoria already knew: it was damn hot! At around three p.m., breaking NEWS interrupted the game to announce that Melbourne had hit a new record temperature of 46.6°C. It was officially an oven in my house and another cold shower was the only remedy to the pending heat stroke that was waiting for me.

Before I could muster up the strength to get off of the couch, my phone began to ring. As I frantically grabbed my phone off of the coffee table, the call display showed a blocked number – meaning it could only be one person.

"Hey Kev," I answered, knowing that it had to be the Fire Depot.

"Get to the yard, mate. Lots of fires going on!" he replied. As soon as I told him that I would be there he instantly hung up. I had received a couple of fire calls from Kev over the past couple of weeks, but this was the first time I could hear stress in his old mumbled voice. Something was not right.

Jumping to my feet, I sprinted outside and got on my pink bike that had been given to me several weeks earlier by one of my fellow firefighters. Pedalling with all of my might, I was soaked head to toe in sweat before I even reached the end of the street. Riding down the 20-metre grass hill that separated my street from the adjacent street below, I picked up momentum as I flew past the park in the centre of town and then veered left through the intersection of Main Street. The houses seemed to blur together as I rode past each one. Sweat constantly rolled down my forehead and into my eyes, causing them to sting. Hot air burned my lungs as I fought for breath while pedalling up the last steep road en route to the Depot.

Before the final descent to the Fire Depot, I happened to glimpse into the distance and what I saw made me stop dead in my tracks. At first, I could see massive cumulus clouds, thicker than I had ever seen, building up from the southwest. These thick, puffy clouds were swiftly gaining in size and starting to take over the pale blue sky in the horizon. Reality instantly set in when I remembered why I was racing on a bike through the small town of Alexandra in the 46°C heat and I realized that those were not threatening clouds on the horizon.

I had no way of knowing that those dark pillars of smoke on February 7th, 2009 would ultimately end the lives of 34 innocent people.

Chapter 1

Leaving Canada

It was the tail end of the 2008 fire season in the wildfire management area of Peace River, Alberta. At that time I had the fortunate pleasure of working for the Government of Alberta as the leader of an initial attack firefighting crew, otherwise known as Helitack. During the preceding warmer months when the lightning would be brave enough to strike the forest, my crew and I would hunt down the fires it created around Northern Alberta. The lightning was now beginning its seven-month hibernation, and so any remaining potential for wildfire was usually caused by overeager farmers or careless campers.

The days had begun to shorten, hinting that winter was just around the corner. This would be my annual cue to initiate my search for where my life would be headed until the next fire season would begin. I had started fighting fires when I was 16, and this would be my ninth winter break from the job that had become such a big part of who I am.

I had come a long way from being the farm boy who had to borrow my father's work boots to go fight two giant forest fires in Washington during my summer break between grades 11 and 12. Little did I know that leaving a note on my parent's kitchen table stating "Gone fighting fires. Had to take your boots, Dad. Thanks" would be the start of the best career I could hope for.

Besides the fact that firefighting is an exciting and satisfying job, I enjoyed the added perk of being able to save enough to travel during the winter months. I wasn't up for humping some crappy restaurant job for five months or going on Employment Insurance, so I had decided early in the summer that travelling would be the route for me, and Australia would be the destination. Australia was a place I had always wanted to go, and so I decided to stop making excuses and make it happen. My older brother had gone there when I was just a kid, and he had told me that it was an amazing place to visit. I was now 24 years old, and it was the perfect time in my life to experience another country and absorb what it had to offer.

During the previous winter, a fellow firefighter named Eben had worked as a Wildland Firefighter in Australia. He had enjoyed his time there so much he was going back for a second fire season, and he suggested that I apply for the job as well. As I had already planned on going there, I couldn't think of a better way to visit Australia than to be working in the field I had come to love. It seemed like a more enjoyable way than fruit picking to spend my time overseas, which was my original plan for collecting income.

I completed the online application form, and with Eben's help and a little luck I was able to get an interview with the

Department of Sustainability and Environment (DSE) in the state of Victoria.

Several weeks after my application was accepted with the DSE, I received the phone call for my interview. "May I please speak to Harold Larson?" said a man with a very thick Aussie accent. It was John Hopper, the fire crew supervisor in the town of Alexandra, Victoria. He was conducting the interview on speakerphone with two other supervisors in that district, Kevin and Dave. Summer was fading fast so I left my room at the Sawridge Hotel to enjoy the warmth of the sun as well as to have the freedom to pace around during the interview.

Their heavy accents coupled with the static coming from the speakerphone made it challenging to understand the questions the three of them had for me. They in turn had a hard time deciphering my Canadian dialect. "Mate, as long as you say yes to all our questions you'll be right," John finally advised after we kept asking each other to repeat what we were saying. The only question I couldn't truthfully say "yes" too was when Kevin asked me if I liked the game of cricket. I had never even seen a cricket match.

They were impressed that I had already purchased a flight ticket to Melbourne and had my working holiday visa in order. I was told that all of the other Canadians that they had hired in the past had left behind good reputations, and I believe that this fact made the interview go as smoothly as it did. By the end of the interview, I had been offered a job in Alexandra as a Wildland Firefighter and was to be in Melbourne by November 25th for a medical exam. I had managed to find year-round forest firefighting employment and this new job would fill my winter perfectly until the next fire season would start again in Alberta.

On November 9th, I boarded my flight with Air Canada at the Calgary airport and left Alberta. After a short layover in Los Angeles, I had a ten-hour flight over the Pacific Ocean before landing in the Cook Islands. As an option with my flight to Australia, I was able to extend any layover for up to a week, and I had decided that a tropical island would be the perfect destination to unwind after the previous fire season. A week of relaxing on white sand beaches and snorkeling in crystal blue waters filled with colourful fish was certainly appealing. I even got to see my first cricket match, which I found entertaining. On November 18th, I hopped back on an airplane and finally arrived in Melbourne.

Jetlagged and groggy from the time change and the long flight, I picked up my two backpacks and proceeded to the customs counter. "So, how did you hear about Australia?" a blonde security woman asked as she opened up my passport.

"I saw it on a map once," I replied with as straight of a face as I could hold. At first I had assumed she was joking, but her emotionless, unblinking facial expression gave no hints as to the point of her question. After a few awkward seconds, I gave her the rundown on my new job and what it all entailed. I also had to let her see my booking for the hostel I was going to stay at. Once my strange interrogation was completed, my passport was stamped and I was free to enter this new country.

I hopped on the shuttle bus that led to downtown Melbourne in search of my hostel. The city of Melbourne is located on the southern tip of Australia right beside the ocean. This modern metropolis is beautiful and trendy, but also crammed with a copious amount of people. After spending the last six months in remote camps, it was almost overwhelming for me to be around so many people. I spent three nights at the Flinders

Station Hostel meeting other travelers and touring around the city. When Eben arrived in Melbourne, we stayed at his friend's apartment and spent the next several days touring the city and visiting popular tourist attractions such as the Sky Deck and the Old Melbourne Jail.

During our last day in the city, Eben and I decided that it would be beneficial for us to purchase computers before we left for the country. It would be more affordable to keep in contact with my friends and family online than it would be through calling cards. The only problem with buying technology here was that the price was far higher than back home. I did not want to spend the hefty amount attached to a laptop, and so I settled for a bulky desktop. After purchasing this monstrosity that was being passed off as a computer, Eben and I parted ways. He was about to start his firefighting job in the small town of Ovens. After we said our farewells, I took a taxi to a medical office where I was to meet up with John Hopper.

Unfortunately, I ended up getting the worst cabbie in Melbourne and was dropped off several blocks from my destination. With my two backpacks strapped on and a large box containing my computer in my arms, I made the grueling walk in the humid heat to the medical office. Dropping my oversized gear on the ground, I rifled through my backpack in search of my towel. I hoped to compose myself before meeting my new boss. While wiping off the sweat that was running down my face, I heard my name being called. Looking up I saw two middle-aged men sitting on a patio at the adjacent restaurant.

"I take it you're Harold," said the stockier of the two men as he stood up and stretched out his arm for a handshake. "I'm John. Nice to finally meet you," he chuckled as he grasped my hand. His grey hair and rounded chin reminded me of Jay Leno. "Sure did bring a lot of stuff from Canada."

The other man stood up, introduced himself as Dok, and explained how he was also here for the medical exam. At first, I was shocked to hear that he had been hired on as a new firefighter – not only because of his age, but also due to his resemblance of a hardened biker. Attached to his weathered face was a long white beard that had a golden hue as it filtered the afternoon sun. Both of his arms wore full tattooed sleeves that showcased skulls, marijuana leaves, and a swastika.

As we sat at the patio table and got to know one another before our scheduled exams started, it was easy to see how cheerful and genuine both men were. John had always been involved in forestry or fire in some capacity and had moved up through the ranks of the government. Dok had been a professional tree faller his whole life and wanted a change of pace in the final years of his working career.

The pre-employment medical exam started off by having me fill out some medical history paperwork. After I handed in my completed paperwork to the receptionist, I was escorted to a doctor's office where an older man asked me a series of health-related questions. He measured my height and weight and administered hearing and vision exams. He looked into my ears and mouth while mumbling comments like "very good" and "no issues here." I had to undergo a succession of range of motion tests that included putting my arms behind my head while trying to touch my elbows and moving my head from side to side. I also had to provide a urine sample to test for something that wasn't explained to me. The whole process took about 45 minutes, and after it was all said and done I had passed with no difficulties.

Dok had some issues passing due to drinking a Red Bull right before his exam, so they had to let his caffeine levels drop before he could get retested. After he passed his second medical exam, we loaded up into John's work truck and headed northeast out of the city.

John decided that we would take the scenic route through the Black Spur in order to get to Alexandra. The Black Spur was a windy road that crept through a mountain range covered with a massive old growth forest that had survived the fires of 1926. Ancient eucalypts, messmates, and giant tree ferns that had watched centuries come and go towered over the steep slopes like colossal sentinels. After we had made it through the Black Spur, the lush green forest gave way to rolling hills of cured grass and brown paddocks speckled with the occasional farmstead.

After an hour and a half of driving, we arrived at the place I would call home for the next several months.

Chapter 2

Alexandra

The rural town of Alexandra had a population of just over 2000 people and served as the hub for the smaller communities in the surrounding area. At first glance, this town that was nestled amongst the parched rolling hills wasn't overly aesthetically pleasing to the eye. This region was on its eighth consecutive year of drought, which had caused the land to become bone dry. The colour palate of the land was limited to a small range of dismal greens and dull browns. A creek that had once flowed through the centre of town was now dried up and hadn't held water in years. Wildflowers were scarce, although some of the gardens in town exhibited a wide variety of exotic plants with colourful blossoms. Large trees lined the streets and roadsides, helping to shade the residents from the heat. It was commonplace to see kangaroos bounding along the hillsides and fields around the outskirts of Alex.

The main industry in this part of Victoria was farming, and the town supplied everything a farmer would require. The town didn't have any well-known businesses or major food chains, though it offered everything one would need such as a grocery store, a hardware store, several bakeries, two banks, and four pubs. I was told that back in the early gold mining days this town was so busy that it had over 30 saloons and pubs.

Being there seemed like a completely different world to me. The subtle differences in how people acted, and the climate, vegetation, and animals were unlike anything I was used to. Even the way the sun was positioned in the sky was different. Having spent the majority of my life outside I had become accustomed to using the sun as a reference point to find cardinal directions. Having to relearn which direction was north without a compass was another unforeseen challenge that at times I found frustrating.

My first stop in Alexandra was to the Fire Depot with Hopper and Dok. The Depot was located at the east end of the town and contained an office, a huge warehouse, a wash bay, a tanker truck area, and other miscellaneous shops. The property was surrounded by a chain link fence with several eucalyptus trees scattered along the fence line and dried out lawn. The brown and yellow buildings that had been bleached by the sun gave me the impression that this Depot had been here for more than a few years and was in need of some renovations.

After the tour of our new workplace was complete, Hopper took us to the equipment shed to get us geared up. We were supplied with a "tradies" uniform that consisted of an orange long-sleeved shirt with blue pants that were to be worn for everyday work. All tradesmen or "tradies" in Victoria have to wear similar looking uniforms while on the jobsite.

I was also issued a heavy two-piece green uniform that was only to be worn while fighting fires. These green uniforms were made out of a thick fire-resistant material called Proban that in my opinion is far inferior to the lighter Nomex material I was used to wearing back home. Wearing those green uniforms felt as if a thick wool blanket was draped around me. We were each issued blue chainsaw chaps as well as other standard work gear including steel-toe boots, a white hardhat, and the stereotypical tan-coloured short shorts that I had seen Australians wearing on television.

Since the place I was moving into wasn't completely furnished, I was also given a cot to substitute as a bed. That army cot was brutal to sleep on and I was thankful when I received a second-hand bed a couple of weeks later from a co-worker.

That evening I moved into the house where I would live for the next four months. Hopper had found this house and had kindly made the living arrangements for me. Two other bachelors were living there and needed another roommate to help pay the bills. My rent was $80 a week, which included power and water.

The one-level house was located on the other side of town from the Fire Depot. It wasn't new by any means but was well kept with three bedrooms, two bathrooms, and a decent backyard covered in patchy brown grass. My room was located at the back of the house which had a separate entrance from the rest of the place. Allegedly, the previous resident of that room had continuously had women going in and out of that entrance which he had deemed the "doggie door". The view from the front door overlooked the town cemetery that occupied the property across the street. This serene graveyard featured far more empty plots than final resting places which were adorned with tombstones and artificial flowers.

Dane, the longest-running tenant of our house, was a Victoria Forester who worked in the head office with Hopper. His 6'2" frame held his 240 lbs, a head crowned with spiky blond hair, and a five o'clock shadow that never disappeared from his round face. He was constantly in a jolly mood and laughed at everything.

My other roommate, Burkie, being short and small, had the opposite build of Dane. The only thing they seemed to have in common was their blond hair. Burkie's quiet nature disguised the tough divorce he was going through. He was often away from the house, but when he was there his two young sons were usually with him.

In the backyard lived Max, an enormous red bull mastiff. Max was a gentle beast weighing well over 100 lbs. This giant dog belonged to Dane and it was apparent how much they loved each other.

The house rules were the same as anywhere else I had ever lived: clean up after yourself, pay rent on time, be respectful, and so on. However, the four-minute shower water usage restriction would take some time for me to get used to.

Once I was settled into the house and introduced to my new roommates, Dane took me to a barbeque in the nearby town of Yarck, a small farming community outside of Alexandra. The barbeque was held in the backyard of his friend's house that also doubled as a convenience store. There I was introduced to gourmet meat pies (tasty salted meat stuffed into a pastry shell) and cricket that we played in the backyard.

The following morning I headed to the main sports field located in the middle of town to prepare for the fitness test. This test was comprised of wearing a 50 lb weight vest and fast walking a distance of three miles in less than 45 minutes. This distance was equivalent to just over 14 laps around the turfed oval. It doesn't sound that grueling, but the kicker is that I was not allowed to run because one foot always had to be touching the ground. This is to simulate the rule that no one should ever be running on the fireline, only walking as fast as possible. Though this rule may sound silly, the most frequent injuries to a firefighter are caused by slips, trips, and falls. Removing the need to run on the fire line, except in emergency situations, helped to diminish these types of frequently occurring accidents.

The fitness test in Alberta had consisted of three parts: the walk previously mentioned, 18 upright rows with a 52 lb barbell, and an intensive pump-hose relay. By this point I had been successfully completing the Alberta fitness test twice a year for several years, so I was confident in my ability to pass.

Four others were also attempting the fitness test. Hopper and Dok were among those as well as another middle-aged gentleman. The fourth was a taller, thin man named Steve who was close to my age with a full head of dark dreadlocks. Everyone who works for the DSE who wants to fight a wildfire has to pass this fitness test, even if their primary role is in the office and not in the field.

After I signed the required medical documents, two of the men supervising the test gently placed the weight vest on me. They repeatedly asked if the vest felt secure or if I was feeling any discomfort. This help and level of attention differed from how it was back home, where I had usually been given a rubber backpack filled with 50 lbs of sand that bounced off my tailbone as I walked the three miles. I was wondering why putting on this weight vest required this high amount of attention until I took another look at the other men who were attempting the fitness test with me. I imagined myself 30 years older and considered how much more difficult this would be. I'm sure the three older men were appreciative of the extra assistance they received.

The five of us lined up at the starting point waiting to begin our 14 laps around the grassy oval. I threw in my earphones and cranked my iPod up for some extra motivation. As soon as one of the supervisors gave us the signal to start, I took off at a relatively fast pace. The key to finishing with a good time was to pace yourself correctly right from the start. It is easier to keep a steady stride throughout the test than to try and speed up during the final laps. I must have been a little overeager to impress my new coworkers, because right away I was told to slow down or else not be allowed to continue. Not wanting to get disqualified, I reduced my speed to a more comfortable pace and continued to truck along.

As we started to knock off laps, black cockatoos soared above giving an aerial display that was a pleasant distraction from the burning in my legs. Birds that resembled magpies mocked us from the sidelines with their auto-tuned sounding calls.

By the time I had finished my tenth lap I was coming up on Hopper's and Dok's heels and was threatening to lap them. "This isn't the commonwealth games, Mate," remarked Dok as I came up beside them.

I responded with only a smile and quickened my jaunt, leaving them behind me.

37:04 was my official time as I completed my 14th circuit, giving the others just under eight minutes to complete the rest of their laps. Throwing off my sweat-soaked weight vest, I sat in the shade and cheered on the others as they continued with the remainder of the test. By the time 43 minutes had past, the last person had walked across the finish line.

I was happy to see everyone pass that day and was looking forward to my new job as a Wildland Firefighter with the Department of Sustainability and Environment.

Chapter 3

Camp Krusty

The last stage of my recruitment before I could be considered an accredited DSE firefighter was to complete a five-day training camp. That year there would be 26 new recruits from all over the Hume district looking to receive their fire certification. Nine of these recruits were from my home area of Alexandra, one of the five areas that made up the Hume district, with seven being firefighters and two belonging to Vic Forests. The Vic Foresters' primary role was to look after timber harvesting operations, but they were also required to be firefighting certified in case of a busy fire season.

The camp that would be our home for the week was located at the Glen Star Resort in the small town of Bonnie Doon. This hamlet is best known for being the movie set where the popular Australian comedy *The Castle* was filmed. I was told that this town had once been a popular tourism destination until the drought had dried up the river that formerly flowed through it. Without the river, tourism had become non-existent and the money that was associated with it had become as scarce as the river itself.

Arriving on site I realized the word "resort" was used loosely here. This place looked more like a rundown farm than a vacation destination. I could tell that at one point this place might have been a hot spot for a summer retreat, but the apparent lack of upkeep had clearly taken its toll over the years. The dilapidated tennis court had more cracks in the cement than were worth counting, each fully occupied with various grasses and weeds. A tarnished chain link fence that surrounded the court was only half intact with the remainder pushed into the corners. The pool that was located in front of the main building was packed full of floating debris and algae.

The main building was of simple design and was painted grey with dark red trim. The ground level was comprised of a reception desk and a restaurant where we would have all of our meals over the duration of the training. The upstairs conference room was used for all of our class sessions.

A string of rooms located in the outside buildings housed two people in each room. My roommate was Nick, an eighteen-year-old Tasmanian who was the youngest employee in our area and in the camp. His front left tooth had been broken in half by a cricket ball which gave him a redneck look, or "bogan" as they like to say. He was always joking around and loved to get on the piss which translates to loves to have a drink. Back in Alexandra he lived in a hotel room in the upstairs of the Commercial pub, which made him a common sight at my favourite drinking hole.

This "resort" had an array of farm and exotic animals running around that included goats and peacocks. The one male peacock continually did its best to impress its female suitors with an elaborate display of shaking its tail feathers while making a loud racket. This mating ritual quickly lost its luster after I started to lose sleep due to its never ending mating calls all night and morning. Throughout the day, kangaroos would hop down to the dugout to drink its muddy water as they battled the high temperatures. I didn't venture too close to the dugout because of the foul stench coming from a dead, bloated kangaroo that was floating in the water. Red and blue rosellas, a small species of parrot, lined the branches of the trees and added colour to the simple brown and green scenery.

The first day was used more for orientation and introduction than for training purposes. We were given time to settle into our rooms and meet everyone that we would be spending the next week with. Most of the recruits, varying in age from 18 to 58, had come from different backgrounds and work experiences. A handful of instructors and knowledgeable firefighters also stayed with us throughout the duration of the course.

I was pleased to find out that I was not the only foreigner to be attending the training. Josh, a Vic Forester from Alexandra, had come from Zimbabwe to start a new life in Australia. We immediately bonded by discussing the Australian culture and observing how it differed from our own. I was extremely fascinated to learn that he had been raised in a polygamist family, a fact which became the topic of several interesting and enlightening conversations. I once asked him if he ever wanted more than one wife. "No my friend, one wife is hard enough to keep happy," he answered with a sly smile.

After the first day's events had been wrapped up, we all made our way to the restaurant for dinner. To everyone's delight, a small bar attached to the restaurant sold drinks for only three dollars each. My fellow rookies loved to drink and have a great time, which was not so different than my training camp back in Canada. Located outside of the pub's back door was a moderate-sized patio that became a great place for me to socialize with my fellow colleagues. When the sun set behind the rolling hills, little white lights strung along the patio railing would light up, adding to the ambiance.

That first evening at Camp Krusty, I joined everyone outside the bar and took up a seat on the patio railing that stood about two metres above the shrub garden. As I was having a conversation with one of the guys about Canadian basketball, I noticed one of the girl rookies looking at me from the patio entrance. When the brunette with green eyes saw that I was looking back at her, she picked up her drink and walked over to me. She introduced herself as Bonnie and tapped my beer with her Can of Bundy, a very sugary mix of premade rum and coke.

"Mind if I take up a seat beside you?" she asked.

"Not at all," I replied as I slid over, giving her room to sit down beside me.

The railing I was sitting on was high enough that my feet were several inches from the patio deck. Bonnie was a fair bit shorter than I am, so she had to make a good sized hop to get her butt up beside mine. She put her back to the railing, braced her hands on the top of it, and hopped up. She must have already had a few cans of Bundy's because instead of jumping onto the railing, she completely overshot it. Her instinct to stop herself from falling over the other side of the railing was to grab the closest object in her reach, which happened to be me. I had nothing to brace myself on but air, so when she grabbed me, I got pulled behind her as we both went backwards off of the railing. As we fell, my one hand was holding a beer while the other was pinned under her. There was nothing I could do but take the full brunt of the fall into my back. Luckily for Bonnie, I broke her fall and luckily for me, the ground broke mine. I was more scraped up than hurt, but it did gain me sympathy points with Bonnie. She was completely embarrassed and tried to make it up to me by buying me drinks the rest of the night as we got to know each other. She was the first girl to literally fall for me. That "fall" would be the catalyst for our friendship that would develop over the next several months.

The next three days were comprised of classroom exercises, lectures, and training sessions in the field. I found the classroom lectures difficult to enjoy, mostly due to the monotone droning of the head instructor. This older gentleman had a way of speaking that was so dry it made the teacher from *Ferris Bueller's Day Off* seem exciting. It took a lot of energy and focus to stay awake and attentive during his classroom sessions. On more than one occasion I would look around the classroom just in time to see someone's head snapping back or forward from falling asleep. Thankfully the majority of the other instructors were entertaining as well as experienced, which helped to mitigate the chore of sitting through those mind-numbing lectures.

Two of my favourite instructors were Mick and Craig. Mick was a shorter man with a cropped auburn beard who worked full time as a firefighter trainer throughout the State of Victoria. I was amused at how his purple shirt matched his purple sunglasses. Craig, who worked for Vic Forests out of the Alexandra depot, was charismatic, and his readiness to help made him an approachable and reliable trainer.

I found the fire behaviour lecture informative and enjoyed learning about the differences in how fire burnt in this landscape compared to the Northern Boreal which I was accustomed too. There were three major factors that stood out to me that differentiated the two fire regimes: availability of water, organic surface layer, and volatility of the vegetation.

In the ecosystems that dominate the central areas of Victoria, there is a limited water supply compared to the abundance of lakes, creeks, and sloughs in Northern Alberta. The majority of the Australian forest floor was covered only by sparse shrubs, fern-like bracken, and the dried up leaves that had fallen from the trees. This type of ground litter was completely opposite from the deep moss and muskeg that dominated the Canadian north. The oily leaves and stringy bark from the eucalyptus trees caused the fire to burn hotter and spread at an alarming rate. All of these contributing elements forced me to change the way I had learned to fight fires. I would have to adopt new tactics and strategies and learn to use different firefighting equipment if I was to be a successful Aussie firefighter.

Fire in any country is driven to spread in certain directions by either wind, slope, or spotting. Fire burns in the direction of the wind creating a head, two flanks, and a back. The head is the hottest and the fastest spreading part of the fire, the flanks burn parallel to the wind, and the backing fire burns against the wind and has the lowest fire activity. If the wind suddenly shifts, turning one of the flanks of the fire into the head, this is when firefighters can find themselves in extreme danger.

Fire also burns faster uphill due to the top of the flames drying out the fuel upslope and creating better burning conditions.

Spotting is the term used when an ember, fire brand, or other heat source is carried by the wind to create another fire apart from the main fire. Spotting here took on a whole new meaning for me compared to what I was used to. The stringy bark eucalypt trees can carry embers in the wind up to several kilometres ahead of the main fire, which results in another difficult element when fighting a fire.

Those three factors need to be considered when directly attacking a fire in order to keep yourself and your crew safe.

Another example of the differences between my previous fire training and the training provided here was apparent after one of the instructors asked the class: "What are examples of safety zones you could utilize if a fire was threatening to burn you over?" Such answers as "a dozer guard" or "a clearing with no vegetation" were suggestions which the instructor agreed with.

I raised my hand and offered the solution, "Go to an abundant water source."

"Can you say that again?" asked the instructor with a confused look.

I thought he was having a hard time understanding my accent so I repeated my answer, making sure to clearly pronounce each syllable: "Go find a body of water or a sufficient water source."

"No. Get into the black," he said, referring to an area that has already been burnt. Using the black as a great backup safety zone was also standard practice for back home. With the vegetation already consumed, the fire behaviour would be reduced in comparison to an area with live fuels. Mostly because of my embarrassment, I didn't follow up as to why he thought it was a bad idea to find water in case of a potential burn over. I imagine he didn't want us looking for water when little could be found in the case of an actual escape scenario.

Training during the third day was held outside in one of the nearby fields. This day was dedicated to learning about the different types of fire equipment and vehicles.

A noticeable difference in equipment was their preference for the rake-hoe: a half-rake, half-hoe combination made out of a 12" x 8" piece of metal attached to a five-foot wooden handle. One side was flat and sharpened and could be used for digging, scraping, and cutting. The other side was made up of 8 to 10 rounded metal spikes that were 4" long. This hand tool was ideal for clearing away debris while constructing a hand line or flipping over burning stumps and logs.

The pulaski, a half-axe, half-hoe hand tool favoured by North American firefighters, was neither shown nor talked about.

The two firefighting vehicles that we used were the slip-on and the tankers. The slip-on was a two-person fire truck kitted out with various firefighting equipment. The make and model of the trucks varied from one area to another and in Alexandra we were fortunate enough to have a fleet of white V8 Toyota Land Cruisers. The box of these trucks held a small pump with 30 metres of rubber hose that was attached to a 400 litre water tank. A fire foam injection kit could be utilized with the water in the event the foam would be needed for structure protection or guard reinforcement. Usually two drip torches, canisters filled with a 50/50 mix of gasoline and diesel, could be used for prescribed burning or back burning purposes. A steel lockbox was welded to the back of the box that housed our chainsaw, axe, fuel, and personal gear. Two rake-hoes were mounted on the underside of the box that could be removed by sliding out a pin that held them to the truck. A bull-bar was fabricated to the front of the truck to help protect the hood and engine from suicidal kangaroos that would occasionally jump in front of moving vehicles. These small, versatile vehicles were perfect for this type of country. They had a huge amount of torque that was needed to climb the steep, rocky tracks that lined the hillsides. They contained enough power to haul a fully loaded trailer, and could even drive through water up to four feet deep. Every slip-on was similar but slight variations made each one unique.

The big brother to the slip-on was the tanker truck. This larger, three-axle truck that was usually painted bright red required an advanced driver's licence in order to operate. The tankers, which were not as big as the city fire trucks, were built to withstand the rural environment. They were equipped with two large water tanks that could hold a combined volume of 3800 litres. Sprinklers were mounted on either side of the cab that could be turned on in the event the truck was trapped in a fire. We were taught to not let the water volume in the tanks drop below 500 litres while on a fire in case the fire blew up. Several pumps and hoses located throughout the tanker could be used in various ways to deliver water to the fire. Up to six firefighters could be riding in and on the tanker at once, but the DSE rarely ever operated with more than two men at a time. The Country Fire Authority, the state firefighting volunteer organization which everyone and their dog belonged too, always seemed to have their tankers filled to the brim with people.

Each night after dinner, everyone would congregate on the patio outside the bar. We would discuss the lessons we had learned that day and I would do my best to answer questions about the differences in how the job was done back home. The Aussie accent was easy to understand and after a while I stopped noticing it; however, the slang that constantly poured from their mouths was a different dialect of English in itself. Dok would take it upon himself to try and decipher what the hell they were saying. For example, "pass the dead horse" is another way to ask for ketchup. Apparently, dead horse and tomato sauce, the Aussie version of ketchup, sound the same to them. "Fair dinkum" was hard for Dok to translate. It's comparable to insisting "I swear it's true" about something far-fetched.

Of course our last night there was spent celebrating the completion of the course. We didn't need a reason to drink, but it was as good of an excuse as any. As the beer bottles started to pile up in the trash can, the music on the stereo was turned up and the work talk transformed into personal conversations and then eventually into a party. Everyone got together and played a couple of games of tipsy backyard cricket in the decrepit tennis courts. One of the recruits brought out his bull-whip to see who could make it crack the loudest.

I tried to wear the Canadian flag on my back and represent my country, but there was no way I could keep up with the Aussies' drinking skills. I was told it would just be un-Australian to not get lit-up, so I joined in the festivities and pounded back more beer than I should have.

Strong bonds are always created with new recruits when they train together and share in the hopes of what the summer has in store. We would all start on Monday as accredited Australian firefighters.

Chapter 4

The Depot

When I arrived at the Depot for my first official day of work, I was surprised to find everyone huddled around an old barbeque watching one of the firefighters fry up breakfast. At the beginning of each fire season, the Alexandra firefighters put on a breakfast BBQ to welcome the rookies to the Depot. The breakfast of bacon, eggs, and kangaroo sausage was an excellent treat for my first day of work. The roo tasted exactly like I thought it would taste: like rabbit but a little tougher to chew.

I was met with handshakes and introductions from the men and women who I would be working alongside for the upcoming fire season. They made a good first impression with their friendly greetings and somewhat humorous jokes. Most of them shared with me some obscure fact about Canada that they knew to break the ice and start up a conversation. A couple of them had been to the West Coast working as white-water rafting guides and told me how much they had loved their time there. Right away they made me feel as if I belonged and was already part of the team.

It was during this BBQ that I met Kevin for the first time. This burly man in his 60s had been fighting fires his whole life and was now in charge of the firefighters who worked at the Depot. When we shook hands during our introductions, his massive, calloused hand dwarfed mine in comparison. It made me wonder about how much damage those banana mitts must have caused on fires back when Kevin had been in his prime. His old, muffled voice along with his thick Aussie accent made it hard for me to understand a lot of what he talked about, and until I got used to his unique speech I usually had to ask someone else what he was saying.

Once the barbeque was finished, Kev gave the rookies a tour of the Depot. He took us inside the main warehouse where we were each assigned a locker. These two-foot by three-foot wooden lockers would be used to store all of our work gear or whatever else we felt necessary that we didn't want to keep at home. We didn't have to worry about locking them, since the warehouse would be closed after hours. And we all trusted the unwritten rule that your fellow co-workers wouldn't look through your work gear. Some of the lockers had elaborate paintings on them depicting different firefighting scenes. Kev's locker displayed a painting of a silhouette of him standing on top of his work truck with a forest fire in the background. To make me feel a little more at home, I taped a Canadian five dollar bill to the front of mine. I was asked on more than one occasion if the blue dollar bill that showed a group of kids playing ice hockey was indeed real. I do suppose some of our currency looks like Monopoly money.

The main warehouse was used to store most of the gear such as the hand tools and chainsaws. It also housed most of the parts we would need to repair any equipment that might get broken. If we wanted a tool or if a piece of equipment needed repairs, we would be responsible for taking care of it ourselves. Having to learn the ins and outs of all of the fire gear helped me become a much more well-rounded firefighter. This was such a refreshing change from what I was used to back home.

In Alberta, a person's only job was to look after the warehouse and all of the precious gear that was hoarded inside. It had been so annoying to try and sign out a piece of equipment, only to have the warehouse person get upset and question why I needed a shovel. How about so I can do my fucking job?

Anyways, after our tour of the Depot was done, we spent the rest of the day in a tiny room filling out paperwork and completing the required safety courses that were needed before we could start working in the field. Especially when you work for the government, the stacks of required certifications, orientations, and safety talks make caffeine a necessity.

The next couple of days were spent in the Depot learning about the chainsaws that we would be required to use on a semi-weekly basis. This training was designed to help us maintain our chainsaws and troubleshoot any problems in the field. It also helped us become knowledgeable enough to fix any major mechanical problems when we got back to the Depot. Unlike Alberta, where any chainsaw with a problem is exchanged at the warehouse for a new one with the broken one sent to a main warehouse to get fixed, here we had to fix any problems ourselves. Having to sort out and repair any issue with the chainsaws increased my mechanical knowledge to a higher level than it would have ever been in Alberta. Plus, I got the added bonus of not having to deal with a warehouse person.

The chainsaws here compared to the ones back home were huge, and I mean huge. Their largest saw, the Stihl 880, had to weigh over 60 lbs and would be impractical for someone to use by themselves. What would be the point of using a saw that required two people to hold it? This saw was over twice the size of the standard issue 365 Huskivarnas that I was accustomed to using. The second largest chainsaw at our disposal was the Stihl 660, and it was still big enough that it was only used when a large project needed to be tackled. My personal favourite was the Stihl 461s. This medium-sized yet powerful chainsaw was the most common to find and I took every opportunity to use this saw whenever I could.

Along with our training, we also had to complete a chainsaw competency test. This informal test required us to go into the field and demonstrate our skills to a couple of instructors. We drove to a spot in the forest and practiced bucking up stumps and tree limbs. Some of the rookies who had previous chainsaw experience showed off their skills by cutting stumps or logs into small chairs and tables. Most of the wood, especially the iron bark, was an amazingly hard and heavy wood. At first, I was frustrated with the amount of time it took to cut through anything. The hardest wood to cut in Alberta is the Birch, yet it shouldn't take more than a minute to cut through a decent-sized stump. Quickly I had to learn the patience required to cut through this extremely hard wood that took about five times the amount of effort than what I was used to. I was also impressed at the massive size and girth of the mature eucalyptus trees. I was able to stand inside one of these giant trees that had its base burnt out from a previous fire with both my arms outstretched and was still not able to touch the sides.

There was no written or scored chainsaw test, but with my previous experience and from what they saw from my two days of sawing they were satisfied enough with my skills to make me a certified Australian bucker and limber. This meant I could cut anything, as long as it wasn't a standing tree. Even though I was a licensed faller in Alberta, I did not receive my tree falling licence in Alex. Very few of the firefighters were faller certified because of the higher skill level that was needed when falling such large, heavy timber. At that point in my career I wouldn't have been comfortable cutting down those giant trees anyways. With their sheer weight and size, it would have been more than a challenge for me.

When I had finally completed all of my training and paperwork, my work routine began to set in as I waited for my first fire call. From Monday to Friday I would wake up at up at six-thirty a.m. and complete the 20-minute walk to the depot. Before the workday would officially begin at eight a.m., I would have to stop by Kev's office and check the white duty board. This duty board posted everyone's name, their project work for the day, and their assigned vehicle. There were no set crews that we worked with on a daily basis. We worked mostly in groups of two to four, but never alone due to work safe practices. This system was different than what I was used to, but it was good to be able to work with everyone and to get to know each of my co-workers before we had to work on the fire line together.

The majority of the full-time firefighters also had a skill or a trade that made them a more valuable asset to the Department. Some were skilled in operating heavy machinery such as the dozers and graders. This made them important when creating fire breaks or maintaining the dirt roads that ran throughout the bush. Some specialized freighters had more than one skill such as Pep, our welder/dozer operator; and Shark, our carpenter/bridge builder. Since I didn't have any specialized skills that they wanted to utilize apart from firefighting, I was mostly used a mule doing manual labour on project days.

The wage we were getting paid was far below what one would except for this job. I was making just over $16/hour with the standard increases for overtime. There was also a 45% wage increase while we were on the fire line. This seemed like a good bonus, but most years working on fires consisted of only about 25% of our working hours. I had a couple of weeks when it was very hard to make ends meet with the paycheques I was getting. Fortunately, for me it wasn't about the money. This was a lifestyle I enjoyed and derived satisfaction from. If I wanted to make a ton of money fast, I would have stayed in Alberta and worked on the oil rigs. But I did feel for the guys I worked with who had to support families on this wage. A lot of them had to work a second job in order to subsidize their income. Some of the older gentlemen had been fighting fires and living this way for over 40 years. I have nothing but respect for the Victorian firefighters for the life they choose to live so they can do the job that they love.

I was very impressed with the Department's work ethic. In this particular workplace, everyone was expected to work hard all day, every day, without complaint. It was almost as if they were competing with each other for a prize that didn't exist. I am not sure if that non-stop work mentality was part of the Aussie culture or if it was contained to this immediate area, but no one was ever late and they all worked harder than any other workforce that I had been a part of. When we were not on fires, the workday consisted of two 15-minute breaks and a 30-minute lunch. Most of the time we would get bored partway through the lunch break so we would cut it short and get back to whatever task was assigned until we had to be back at the Depot for five p.m. My work ethic greatly improved after my time working for the DSE, an improvement for which I will be forever grateful. In Alberta, when the fire hazard is high most of my time is spent waiting beside the helicopter hoping for a dispatch. After seeing how hard everyone worked, I didn't have the heart to tell them that a lot of the time back home I had been just sitting on my ass waiting for a fire to start.

The fire hazard in Alexandra was high most of the time, so even in the grueling hot days we just worked until we got a fire call. Only on our scheduled days off when we got called in would we ever just sit at the Depot waiting for a dispatch.

After my first two weeks there, Eben phoned me and asked how my time was going. I simply replied, "I am working like my visa depends on it." He laughed and said that he could relate to the feeling all too well.

Chapter 5

Project Work

Two weeks had gone by since my arrival in Alexandra and no fires had started. Fires don't burn throughout any region for 365 days a year; therefore, firefighters can't always be fighting a fire. When there is no training to be done and no fires to fight, project work is usually what's on the menu. Because the DSE is a public service, a lot of our work hours were allocated to road and bridge maintenance, noxious weed removal, and park cleanup. Most of the project work that I participated in consisted of track clean-up and park maintenance. Hundreds of dirt roads, walking trails, and prepositioned fire breaks constantly needed upkeep throughout the season in order to make them trafficable.

There are four main State forests in the Alexandra area that we worked in: Blue Range, Black Range, Rubicon, and Big River. Each forest shares the same base species of vegetation and rolling topography, but all are unique in their own way. The ash trees grow amazingly fast in these forests, with some as tall as

20 metres in less than 20 years. These trees would consistently fall over and occasionally block some of the paths and roads, thus keeping us busy with tree removal throughout the season. At times the larger trees, some as wide as a Volkswagen Beetle, would hinder a trail and take a considerable amount of time to clear.

It was a relief to look at the whiteboard for the first time and see an assignment beside my name instead of training. For my first day of work in the field I would be part of a group that was assigned to clean up a public campground by Lake Eildon located 30 km east of Alexandra. Soon all of the kids would be out of school for the upcoming Christmas holidays, and each campsite would be overflowing with campers trying to escape the city for the weekend. This would be the first time I would be going out into the field and working with the experienced firefighters.

For the day I was paired up a man who everyone called Gogo. He had just moved to Alexandra from another work centre in the Hume district. He got this nickname from his inability to sit down due to his tenacious work ethic. He was a thinner man with cropped blond hair and fair skin, colouring which caused him to always have a red glow due to the high UV index. It was commonplace to see him smoking a hand-tailored cigarette that was rolled to perfection. He could even roll his smokes one-handed – that way he could drive and smoke at the same time. Gogo had this hidden talent of stretching out the workday by at least half an hour longer than he was supposed to. He was also by far the most passionate firefighter that I have ever met in both the Northern and Southern Hemispheres.

After I got geared up, I sat down at the picnic table and waited for the rest of the crew to get ready. As I sat there, I suddenly got that feeling that something wasn't right. Scanning the Depot, I couldn't see anything out of the ordinary except for a couple of the rookies staring at me. Looking down, I noticed what looked like a shiny black rope on the ground beside my feet. Suddenly I realized it wasn't a rope; it was a curled up red-bellied black snake, one of the more poisonous snakes found in the area. Quickly jumping to my feet, I did this weird shimmy movement to get some space between me and the snake.

Laughter erupted from the rookies who were watching me. "No worries, Harry; it's a dead one," said Singo, one of the rookies I had gone to Camp Krusty with. Looking back at the motionless snake I could now see that it was clearly dead. Singo had run over the snake on his way to work and thought it would be good fun to give the Canadian a scare by placing it beside me when I wasn't paying attention.

"Very funny, asshole," I replied, trying to not feel embarrassed. It was actually pretty funny, and Singo thought it was golden - until Kev gave him shit about it. That would be the only snake I saw that summer. Maybe I got lucky because I inquired about all the dangerous animals and insects and how best to avoid them, or it could be that I just didn't know what I was looking for.

I jumped in the Land Cruiser with Gogo and left Singo and his snake behind as we drove towards the campground. The amazing drive to Lake Eildon consisted of winding roads that cut a path through the thick eucalyptus forest that surrounded either side. Exotic birds and animals that were all new to me filled the land and trees along the roadside. The guys were always more than happy to point out any new animals or plants that I had not seen before and to share their local knowledge with me. When it came to sharing local knowledge, Gogo was the champ. It was like listening to the Discovery Channel by the amount of facts he would throw at me.

Once we arrived at the campground, we started the process of removing debris and dangerous trees from the different campsites. We repaired damaged or incomplete fire pits and collected any trash that needed to be disposed of.

At one of the campsites there was a flagged-off area about twenty metres square in size. It was flagged to keep the public out so that the forest could have a chance to grow back. In the middle of this area was a three-foot stump on a small mound that Gogo asked me to get rid of. Apparently this stump was an eyesore and its removal was needed for park beautification.

Feeling confident, I retrieved the chainsaw and the appropriate safety gear and got into it. In order to cut the stump right close to the ground, I had bent down on one knee before I started to make my cut. Driving the chainsaw into the wood I began to separate the stump from its base that was flush with the ground. As woodchips flew out from my chainsaw, I noticed something about the size of a drink coaster move under the loose bark of the eucalyptus stump. Getting the same premonition I had gotten in the snake episode that something wasn't right, I pulled out my saw and set the chain break.

Looking more closely, I could see a few other objects also moving underneath the bark. Suddenly the stump came alive with movement as dozens of huge huntsmen spiders started to scurry everywhere. As I was backing away, out of the corner of my eye I noticed something moving on my right shoulder. I turned my head to get a better look and two inches from my face was a massive huntsmen spider reared up on its back legs. This hairy, brown, eight-legged monster was the size of the palm of my hand. In my terror-driven panic, I dropped the saw, did a superman jump off of the mound, and then started doing the scat man dance to clear any and all spiders that were on me. After the guys stopped laughing, they explained to me how the huntsmen are not poisonous and rarely ever bite people. Poisonous or not, it still felt like I had undergone a minor heart attack.

Twice in one day, I had been given the privilege of experiencing Australia's creepy crawlies. I never had to worry about those sort of critters back in Alberta, where the only animals that could cause any concern were bears, cougars, and moose. The majority of Aussies I met liked to ask me about big animals in Canada, mostly due to the fact that they have no native mega fauna of their own. The largest carnivore they have is the Tasmanian devil, a creature that is the equivalent size of a medium dog. Out of all the big creatures in the Canadian north, they were extremely fascinated with bears. Something about a wild animal that was big enough to eat you really seemed to interest them and awake a primal fear that they never had to face. They thought it was crazy to work in the forest with these creatures that have the potential to eat you.

To get back at the guys for the snake episode, I conceived a story that before anyone is allowed to work in the Canadian forests they have to take a two-day hand-to-hand bear combat training course. Although we do have to take a two-hour Bear Aware course on how to avoid bears and what to do if we ever encounter one, no formal combat training is ever given.

With their intense fascination of bears coupled with their lack of experience with carnivorous mega fauna, it was really easy to convince them that bears and people fought on a regular basis. I would tell stories about bear encounters and they would accept them as gospel. When I was in high school my older cousin Dan had been attacked by a black bear close to Prince George, BC. That was one story I didn't need to exaggerate to put the fear of bears into them. To my knowledge, some of the guys still think Canadian forestry employees need to take hand-to-hand bear combat training.

On a different project day, I was tasked to clear a tree that had fallen across one of the dirt roads in the Black Range. This blue gum eucalypt that had once stood close to 70-metres tall was the biggest tree that I had ever seen that needed to be cleared off of a road. The giant had broken right at the stump that was located about five feet on the upwards side of the road, thus causing the tree to fall perpendicular across the road.

For that day I was paired up with Craig, one of my former instructors at Camp Krusty. Once we arrived at the tree, we got out of our truck to examine the fallen giant and to formulate a plan of how we were going to tackle this project. This wasn't some tree that we could just get into and hope for the best; this tree demanded our respect and full attention. The diameter of the tree was so large I could barely see over the trunk to the other side of the road.

"Feel like givin' it a go, mate?" Craig asked after we had stared at it for several moments.

"For sure," I replied with my Canadian slang. Putting on my chaps and grabbing the Stihl 660, we walked around the base of the tree to figure out the best way to cut this beast. The main danger this tree presented was its potential to roll back on me due to its remarkably heavy weight. I also had to make sure the chainsaw bar didn't get stuck in the wood while I made my cuts. If I cut the stump in the wrong spot or in the wrong direction, the cut could pinch in on itself and trap the bar. We only had one chainsaw with us, so if I got the bar stuck we would have to drive back in shame and get another chainsaw to rescue the pinched bar.

With a tree that large and heavy it was hard for us to determine exactly where the compression and tension points were. After ten or so minutes of examining all the angles and possibilities, we decided the best course of action was to start at the base of the tree and work our way towards the top until it would be lying flat on the ground and less likely to pinch the saw. Unfortunately, this meant that I would have to be standing on the high side of the slope beside the road where I would have to balance myself while making cuts at the same time. The 30-inch bar could only reach about a third of the way through the tree, so I had to make my first cut on both sides and then make my final cut through the middle. Once I started to make my cuts, Craig hammered huge aluminum wedges into the openings to keep the wood from pinching in on itself. Adrenaline rushed through me each time I made a final cut, hoping that I had made the right choice in my placement and the cut would go through without pinching or having the tree roll back on me and crush my legs. Each cut took me a substantial amount of time because of its size and how hard the wood was. Slowly but surely I was able to remove enough off of the base of the tree to get off of the slope and cut on a flat surface.

Because of how dense the wood was and how long it took for me to get the tree flat on the ground, I had to sharpen my saw before I could commence on the rest of the huge wooden blockade. Once the tree was lying flat on the road, I made one final cut on the opposite end of the road from where the stump was. That final cut separated the wood on the road from the rest of the tree.

The only thing left to do was to remove the tree from the road. We tried to push the rest of it off of the road so we could roll it down the hillside, but it was too heavy for us mortal men. Cutting the tree into small enough pieces for us to move would take more time than we had left in the workday, so we decided to snig it to the side of the road. Snigging is the process of wrapping a thick chain around the tree and attaching the other end of the chain to the tow bar on the back end of the truck. With the snig in place we pulled the cut section of timber so that the length of the log was parallel with the road and out of the way. Success! From there at least it was out of the way and could be removed later on when some heavy machinery became available. This entire process took us at least a couple of hours from start to finish, and was a fun way to spend the afternoon.

Craig was also my instructor for my 4 x 4 off-road driving training. I had completed an in-class course about off-road driving during training camp, but had very little experience driving in this type of landscape. Not only did I have to learn how to drive on the left side of the road, I also had the added challenge of learning to drive on terrain that I was not used to. It seemed simple enough in my head, but in order to drive in Australia I had to let go of a lot of habits that I had developed during my driving career. Simple tasks such as signaling were now something I had to think about. The wiper and signal handles were on the opposite sides of the steering wheel, and so sometimes when I would go to signal, I would accidentally turn on the wiper blades or vice versa. All of our trucks were standards, and so I also had to learn how to shift with my left hand. The pedal placement was still the same; however, shifting with my left hand was awkward and needed some practice in order to find the gears. Shifting from second to third seemed to be difficult for me. I would constantly jam the bloody shifter in between first and third, which was frustrating. Round-abouts were far more common here than they were in Canada, and they were used instead of four-way stops. At first I didn't have a clue about how to negotiate an Aussie round-about. I would just hazard a guess, hold on to the wheel, say "here we go" in my head, and giv'er. Haz vs. round-abouts: nature's oldest battle.

My off-road training exercises included driving up and down steep rocky tracks that ran along the spur lines in the hills. Picking your lines and the right gear when attempting a steep descent or a climb was a skill on its own. It was quite a rush driving on slopes with a 30% grade. Going up you would see more sky than ground, and going down always felt a lot steeper than what it was. The key was trusting in your abilities and keeping the tires orientated up and down the hill. Whatever you do, don't touch the clutch; just pick a gear and stick with it. If you have to stop on a slope, pull the e-brake and let the truck stall. Pushing in the clutch when the truck started to slow down was a habit I had to break quickly in order to not roll down these steep hills.

During one of the steepest tracks I had ever driven on, Craig pulled up on the emergency brake and stalled the land cruiser. Thanks, Craig. In order to get the truck going again up the track without it rolling backwards, I had to start the truck while the emergency brake was on, let the clutch partially out with just the right amount of gas, and then release the emergency brake slowly. This stall start was effective but also difficult to master and a little scary to perform, as it caused massive clenching.

When I was not clearing roads and practising my driving, I would usually be assigned to clearing walking tracks. Most of the track clearing that we did consisted of removing smaller pieces of timber that could be moved easily, unlike the giants that we had to deal with on rare occasions. The most memorable track-clearing experience occurred when a handful of us tackled the Cathedral Range State Park. The Cathedrals are a clump of hills located west of the Rubicon State Forest. This particular stretch of rocky hills jetted straight out of the ground and towered over the lower hills that surrounded them. The steep vertical slopes that jutted out of the jagged landscape gave them their well-deserved name.

At the base of the Cathedrals, ten of us loaded up our backpacks with water, armed ourselves with rake-hoes and chainsaws, and started our ascent to the top of the mountain by following the steep walking trail that had been etched into the hillside. The mature forest that grew on either side of the track was stunning and full of life; however, the hot and unforgiving weather took away from some of the enjoyment provided by the forest's scenery. Sweat continuously dripped from our helmets, reminding us that we constantly needed to drink water to stay hydrated. We had to trade sawyer duties throughout the crew in order to keep our fatigue to a minimum. The added heat that came with the chaps as well as the extra strain from the chainsaw would be enough to drop anyone after a full day's use in the intense heat. Slowly we cleared the steep track as we climbed up one step at a time.

Those bastard aggressive ants were commonplace along the track. They liked to live in rocky areas and seemed to love using the Cathedrals for their nests. On more than one occasion I would hear someone scream "jumpers!" or "inchmen!"

and watch as they would high-step quickly in the opposite direction from where they were coming from. If a large piece of timber happened to fall on an ants' nest, then that is where that timber would stay.

Halfway up the hill we stopped for a short water break and to relieve some of the lactic acid buildup in our legs. During our break, Gretchy put his head between his knees and breathed heavily while sweat poured onto the ground. "I must be out of shape. I don't remember the climb being this hard," he wheezed. He looked in rough shape and definitely needed this break.

"Look in your pack, mate," one of the guys said from lower on down the track. Grabbing his pack, Gretch opened it up and looked inside. A disgusted look came across his face as he reached inside and pulled out several large rocks that combined must have weighed at least 40 lbs. Earlier in the day a couple of the guys had hid the rocks in the bag when he wasn't paying attention.

"You dicks," was all he could say as the rest of our crew burst out in laughter at the successful prank he had been at the poor end of.

After our break we continued working up the track, clearing anything that was blocking us from our goal of reaching the lookout point where the path ended. Large salamanders scurried through the bracken and under rocks as we disturbed them from their daily routines. After a couple more hours of steadily moving up in elevation, the taller trees turned into shorter gnarled gum eucalypts. The gums' twisted trunks and branches leaned heavily to one side, giving them the appearance of being frozen in time after having been assaulted by gale force winds. Moving through these sub-alpine species we reached the lookout point. The view was breathtaking. All around us the long-standing eucalypts lined the peaks of the Cathedrals. Beneath them old growth forests mixed with a patchwork of pine plantations shimmered in the afternoon sun. The sun was strong, but a cool breeze flowed around us as we enjoyed our lunch on the top of the mountain. Along with the satisfaction of what we had accomplished that day came the gift of this awe-inspiring landscape. That alone was worth the grueling trip up the Cathedrals.

I enjoyed the other aspects of working for the DSE apart from fighting fires. Every day I got to try out new jobs and work with different people on the crew. Through work I travelled parts of Victoria that I would have otherwise never even known existed. My work helped me experience the wonder of the Australian forests that occupy central Victoria.

Chapter 6

Chrissy

For the first time in my life I woke up in an empty house on Christmas morning. It was strange not being around my family during this holiday. On the plus side though, it was also the first time I was able to wear a t-shirt, shorts, and sandals while being outside on the 25th of December with no worries about freezing to death. Christmas is celebrated in Australia, but not to the extent that it is celebrated in Canada. Sweating in the 30°C heat on a hot summer's day is just not the same as huddling indoors before a warm fire, waiting in anticipation for a great feast with snow falling on the windowpanes.

For my first Aussie Christmas I was invited to attend a barbeque lunch at Dash's house in Eildon and then go to Bonnie's house for dinner. Dash was another rookie firefighter who had attended training camp with me. He was the only other person I knew who loved the movie *Young Guns* as much as I did. With our shared affection for that movie, we developed a game where we would try to find the perfect timing to use the movie quotes. Usually this game would cause one of us to burst out laughing in a crowd that had no idea what was going on.

Around lunchtime, Dash swung by my place and picked me up in his red truck. "Merry Chrissy, Haz," said Dash as I got into his truck. "Let's start this off right and get some holiday cheer into us."

By holiday cheer he meant beer, so our first stop was the liquor store called the "Thirsty Camel". Arriving at the store, Dash pulled his truck in front of the shop and someone came out to ask us what we wanted. My first Christmas miracle. My mind was just blown that I was at a drive-thru liquor store. What was even more shocking was there is no law prohibiting open liquor in vehicles, and it is legal for the passengers to drink. Some of the guys I knew even had coolers in the middle console of their vehicles to accommodate this law. The driver's blood alcohol level had to be under 0.05, which at the time was three points lower than in Canada. This seemed to surprise any Aussie when I told them that. We picked up some bottles of Carlton Draught and headed west out of Alexandra.

Taking advantage of this newly discovered novelty, I cracked a beer as we drove down the curvy road towards Dash's house. We stopped at the dam that feeds the Goulburn River from Lake Eildon. This man-made lake supplied the town of Eildon as well as several other communities with water. The years of continuous drought had seen the lake dry up to only 15% of its holding capacity, a fact which caused water restrictions to anyone that used its water. After our short break of basking in the sun, we continued to his house.

Dash gave me a quick tour of his place and then fired up the barbeque. For this special occasion he had bought a tray full of marinated prawns. It was hard not to say "Put another shrimp on the Barby," but let's be honest: it had to be done. Once the prawns were finished cooking, we sat on the porch and ate the delicious morsels accompanied with clams and beer to wash it all down. Dok, who lived just up the street, came over and shared a beer or two with us as we enjoyed the Aussie music on the radio. We had a few laughs as I explained the differences between how the holidays are spent across the Pacific. No need for sunscreen back home. They both agreed that they would never want to experience the cold that arrives every winter in Northern Alberta.

A couple of hours after we had finished eating, Bonnie picked me up from Dashy's house and drove me the hour or so to her mom's farm close to the small town of Toolangi. The farmhouse was located at the end of a very long driveway that snaked through medium–high scrub peppered with the occasional gum tree to hide the house from the main road. The house was older but still held an elegant look for where it was, and it was surrounded by several paddocks full of cattle that Bonnie's family owned and sold for beef.

Once we parked Bonnie's car, I was introduced to her mom and older sister Tessa. Bonnie and her mother shared the same brunette hair while Tess was blonde. It was easy to tell they were related as they shared the same hippie style and a fondness for walking everywhere in bare feet.

For dinner we had a nice spread of different cheeses and vegetables. Bonnie's mother had picked some wild mushrooms earlier in the day and fried them up as one of the side dishes. She explained how she couldn't identify the exact species of mushrooms that she had picked, but was confident they were edible. I was not as confident as this lady who I had met only hours before, so I politely declined the potentially poisonous food I had been offered. Sorry, but like hell I was going to try those.

It was nice spending Christmas with company and not having to be by myself for the holidays. It made the distance from my family seem not so far away. We spent the rest of the evening talking and getting to know each other until we retired for the night.

After Boxing Day breakfast, Bonnie's mom asked if I could help around the farm for a little bit before we headed into Melbourne to visit Bonnie's dad's side of the family. Her brother who also lived on the farm had been away travelling, and so some of the heavy farm work hadn't been completed since he had left. She asked if I could take the chainsaw and cut away brush or trees that had fallen onto any of the fences on the farm. She was worried that if too much timber accumulated on the fence, the fence would lose some of its strength and the cattle could potentially escape.

Of course I wanted to help out, so I grabbed her brother's saw and joined the three women in the farm van. Bon and I jumped in the back while Tess jumped on the hood. "What is she doing?" I asked Bon. Tess stood up on the hood as her mom put the van in drive.

"She's looking for wombat holes. It's really hard to see them in the tall grass, and if we get a tire in one we will get stuck," Bonnie explained.

"Fair enough." I had seen enough bizarre things in the month I had been here to just chuckle and sit back in my seat. Before we got to the sections of fence that bordered the forest, we drove to the middle of the paddock and emptied some bags of grain for the cattle to feed on. A massive bull they called "Dunlop" led the charge as the herd of cattle moved across the paddock for their meal. We drove away before we became surrounded by the hungry cows and arrived at the section of fence that needed our attention.

While Bonnie and I bucked and limbed the fallen trees free of the fences, Tess and her mom walked around the paddock and plucked out any noxious weeds that had taken root on their property. We moved from section to section clearing anything that was needed and removing any trees that had the potential to fall over in the near future.

While we walked from fence line to fence line, Bonnie would entertain me with stories about her life. She had an education in Environmental Science and it was interesting to hear her views on Australian politics or the environmental issues that were currently going on.

It was around lunchtime and the temperature was rising to the point where working in the heat was becoming almost unbearable. The last tree that we removed took quite a bit of time and energy as it was the largest of the bunch and had fallen directly across one portion of fencing. We were out of gas for the chainsaw, and with the sun starting to scorch our skin we decided to call it a day. Bon called out to the other two and signaled for them to join us at the van in our retreat from the relentless sun.

Tired and sweaty, I loaded the chainsaw into the back of the van and sat down in the back seat. As soon as I sat down, searing pain stabbed into my butt cheek. Lurching forward and grabbing my ass, another sting hit me in the backside, then another and another. It felt as if a hornet's nest had been shoved into my pants. "Bees!" I screamed as I jumped out of the van clenching my ass.

"It's ants; hurry, drop your pants," Bon instructed. Before she even finished her sentence I was halfway stripped as she began brushing away the jumping jacks that had somehow made their way into my pants. "Hold still so I can get them," she yelled.

"What's happening?" was all I could say.

After a couple more swats the ants were removed and the stinging was replaced by a throbbing, burning sensation. "I think I got them all," Bonnie said while holding back her chuckles.

While I was adjusting to the pain these little devils had inflicted and to the reality of what had just occurred, I looked up to see Bonnie's mom and sister looking at me. I then looked down to see my pants and underwear still down around my ankles. The stings hurt so much that I could care less if they got an eyeful of Canadian bacon. I was just relieved there were no more ants attacking me. After a few deep breaths I pulled up my pants and composed myself while the three of them shared a laugh - hopefully at the situation, and not at what they had seen.

Besides the danger of snakes and spiders in this country came the added threat of ants that everyone had neglected to mention until after I got bit. In a country where everything is stingy, bitey, and poisonous, why wouldn't the ants be just as hostile? The two species that were a cause for concern were the inchmen and the jumping-jacks. The inchmen are just as the name suggests: about an inch in size, dark brown in colour, and with massive pincers. The jumping-jacks are about half the size of their larger cousins with yellow pincers and a retract-able wasp-like stinger. The jumpers get their name from their ability to quickly jump in any desired direction. Each species shows no fear and will readily attack anything that they feel threatened by. If you were unlucky enough to be stung by one of these little bastards the pain that is associated with them is not forgotten. They like to crawl up your pants, look for a perfect spot, bite into your skin, hold on, and repeatedly sting. Since that encounter with the jumping-jacks I always made sure to avoid the little insects with the painful stings as best as I could.

On the way back to the farmhouse we stopped at the dugout where Bon and I took a refreshing dip in the cool water. It was a good reward for the work that we had just done. The freshness of the cold water seemed to help with the burning from the stings, at least for the moment.

After lunch we parted ways with Bonnie's mom and went to Melbourne where we had an excellent dinner and a great night with the rest of Bonnie's family. Besides the ant episode that had forced me to show off my trouser snake, I had a great Christmas and a memorable holiday Down Under.

Chapter 7

The Hunt

Another week of work was finished and I was settling into my evening routine of making dinner and hanging out with my roommates. While in the process of figuring out what I should do this particular Friday night, I received a call from one of my favourite coworkers.

"Hey mate, how ya going?" Shepard asked in his usual heavy Aussie accent.

"Not too bad," I replied. "Just sweating my ass off as usual. Thinking about heading down to the Commercial for a drink or two. You should come." Shepard and I had spent a couple of nights at the local pub, and over the last couple of weeks he had become more of a friend than a work colleague.

"How you feel about coming hunting later tonight? Ades can swing by your place and give you a lift," he proposed with a hint of excitement in his voice.

"Umm, do I need a hunting license?" I asked.

"No mate, this is Australia!" Satisfied with Shepard's reassurance that everything was a go for hunting, I geared up and packed an overnight bag while I waited for Ades to come pick me up.

Close to seven p.m., Ades showed up with Nick, who had also received an invite to join in the hunt, and we drove 20 minutes west to the neighbouring town of Yea where Shepard lived.

Pulling into Shepard's driveway, the first thing I noticed was his dark blue truck that he loved more than any man could love a woman. Shepard had once tried to explain to me the special bond that is created between man and machine, a bond which I had never fully understood. This medium-sized truck was decked out with everything he would need for an off-road excursion.

Located at the back of the driveway was a fenced in area that housed his two massive dogs. The larger of the two was Loki, a distinguished looking staghound whose back stood thigh high to me. His other dog, a wolfhound named Spike, was broader than Loki and almost as tall. As soon as they were released from their pen they came running out with tails wagging, looking for some attention. I could tell by the way his dogs listened and followed their master that Shepard had spent a great deal of time training and caring for the two of them. Two cages were mounted on the box of his truck. Following Shepard's command, both dogs jumped in.

Before we could leave we were given a tour of Shepard's house and introduced to his parents. They were a nice and sincere couple who shared an intense passion for Clint Eastwood. The more time I spent walking around their house, the more Clint Eastwood paraphernalia I saw. The crown jewel of their collection was a large portrait of their hero painted on a velvet canvas that hung triumphantly in the living room. Following the tour of the unofficial Clint Eastwood museum, we loaded up the rest of the hunting supplies and departed in Shepard's truck to a nearby farm that would be our setting for the hunt to come.

After a short drive away from the town and into the countryside, we pulled up to a rusty gate that led into an open paddock. Shepard wanted to have a tailgate meeting before we continued any further and go over specifics about what the night had in store for us.

With his forehead scrunched, he explained how he had once worked as a farmhand on this property that we were about to go hunting on. The farmer was now having difficulties with the overabundance of kangaroos who were eating everything in his fields and leaving little grazing opportunities for his livestock. "We'll just take out a couple of the big males in each group and anything that's not native to Aus. If you don't get a good shot, no worries: my dogs will take care of the rest," he explained while throwing in a wink. "Just make sure you don't shoot anything local."

A number of introduced species had done and continued to do irreversible damage to the native ecosystems. The mild winters and lack of natural predators had resulted in overwhelming populations of invasive species such as rabbits, feral pigs, and deer that had been brought over by the early settlers. Foxes, who were originally released for sport hunting, had quickly adapted and consequently decimated indigenous small animal populations.

Dogs and cats that had gotten lost or escaped into the woods quickly become feral and ate native birds, fish, reptiles, and small mammals at an unprecedented rate, even to the point of causing the extinction of several species. Packs of wild dogs had been known to kill livestock in the local area. These dogs had become such a growing problem in the area that the Department of Sustainability and Environment had hired a "Dog man" whose sole purpose was to hunt and trap feral dogs and cats. This measure was a culture shock for me, after coming from a country where for the most part all dogs and cats are domesticated. I was sure that if I told someone in Canada that I had killed dogs and cats, they would have wondered about my mental health.

It made no difference how or for what reason these animals were introduced into the landscape. They were wreaking havoc, and so we were instructed to shoot anything not Australian without remorse.

As serious as his scruffy face and heavy jowls would allow him to look, Shepard carefully explained his rules for safe hunting and firearm etiquette. He had brought out three rifles for us to use: a .22 semi sonic, a .22 magnum, and a .308 Remington. The .308 would be used for bigger game such as kangaroos, while the other two rifles would be used for anything else. He was also equipped with a large bowie knife that he had strapped onto his belt as well as a police baton stashed behind the backseat in his truck.

Shepard had made a special addition to his truck in order to hunt at nighttime: a spotlight that could be mounted on the roof and attached to a handle he had fabricated between the driver and passenger seats. This spotlight could then swivel in all directions, giving us even more of an edge in the epic battle between man and nature. It reminded me of the "All-Seeing Eye" in *The Lord of the Rings* movies. I never asked Shepard if spotlight hunting was legal, knowing how irrelevant the question would be.

Once Shepard was satisfied that we understood his instructions, we loaded back into the truck and continued into the paddock. With Shepard driving and me sitting shotgun, Nick and Ades stood in the box of the truck with their firearms at the ready. We must have looked like such a bunch of rednecks.

The first animal that we came across was a wombat scurrying over the stubby grass. This furry black animal moved remarkably fast for how short its legs were. Before this, the only wombats I had seen were the dead ones that weren't fast enough to dodge traffic on the highways.

As the daylight started to disappear and finding prey was becoming progressively harder, we turned on the "All-Seeing-Eye" and continued driving in search of our first casualty.

Shining the spotlight through the trees, a set of golden eyes reflected back at us. Driving closer we saw that the eyes belonged to a koala who was relaxing in a nook of a hefty eucalypt. It paid us little attention as it continued to chew on its late night snack of leaves.

Suddenly Shepard stopped his truck and pointed the spotlight at the crest of a nearby hill. Out of the darkness, a mob of illuminated kangaroos came bounding towards us. Before I could ask what the plan was, Shepard got out of the truck, pulled out his .308, and blasted one of the bigger roos. He hit it directly in its chest, dropping its lifeless body to the ground. This caused the other roos to panic and flee in the opposite direction.

"That's how it's done, mate," he said out of the corner of his mouth while still looking through the scope of his gun.

"Wow, this is Australia," I said to no one in particular.

After congratulating him on his great shot we noticed another mob coming over the neighbouring hillside. "You're up, Haz," Shepard said as he handed me the rifle.

I took the .308 and lined up a roo through the scope that was standing about 70 metres away. Aiming the crosshairs right at the roo's heart, I slowly let out my breath and fired. Though I hit it directly in the chest, instead of the roo falling over dead it slumped forward and sluggishly started to crawl towards the scrub as the rest of its mob scattered into the darkness. After this disappointing shot, Shepard went to the back of his truck and let his two dogs out of their cages. "Go get em," he instructed while pointing in the direction of the kangaroo who was living in struggletown.

"Release the hounds!" Nick shouted as the large dogs raced towards their injured prey. I was expecting them to instantly rip the roo apart, but instead the dogs just circled the roo who was now paralyzed with fear.

With Shepard's hand resting on the handle of his bowie knife, he stoically walked over to the terrified roo, grabbed one of its legs, and methodically pulled out his knife and stabbed the roo in its lungs. While he was putting the roo out of its misery, it gave one final attempt to escape and kicked out its hind leg that Shepard was holding onto. Then he went motionless. This sudden kick left Shepard's shoulder incredibly sore and we could clearly see the pain on his face as he muttered curses through his clenched jaw.

Due to the combination of Ades' and my distaste for what had just happened and Shepard's new injury, we decided to find some smaller game to pursue. We got back into our same positions – Shep and me in the truck with the other two in the box – and left the open paddocks. We drove towards a rocky outcrop that Shepard knew from past experiences was a haven for rabbits. As we rolled in the direction of this new hunting grounds, I asked Shepard how he felt about the animals that didn't die right away. I wondered if it bothered him. "No worries, mate. I've killed hundreds and they don't always go down all nice and pretty," he reasoned.

I pointed the spotlight along a loose barbwire fence and spotted a small dog lurking alongside the fence line. "It's a fox. Get it, Ades!" Shepard yelled out of his window. Ades quickly fired his rifle and missed. The fox was clearly confused, because it ran straight for the truck. Firing the rifle a second time, Ades hit and killed the fox only 20 metres away from us.

"Nice shot," I shouted to Ades as the two in the box cheered in unison. Shepard was just relieved that Ades hadn't shot a hole in the hood of his truck as the fox had come running towards its impending doom. Killing this fox was a huge victory for my three hunting companions, and their elation showed me just how important killing these pests were. With one invasive killer removed from the population, the fox with the bullet hole through its back was thrown into the bushes and we continued to the rocky outcrop.

Over the next hour, several rabbits made the mistake of appearing in our proximity, and Nick and Ades had no problem shooting them. We all took turns driving and taking aim at the furry critters as they ran for cover. Shepard was an amazing shot and rarely missed his mark. The rest of us were pretty average but good enough to get the job done most of the time. Seventeen rabbits would never see another sunrise after our patrol of their home, and a couple of them would become meals for the two dogs in the back.

Satisfied with the amount of pests we had eradicated, we decided to start our journey back home. Shep and Nick jumped into the box of the truck with hopes of shooting another roo before the hunting trip was over. Shepard wanted to show off his marksmanship, so when we found another mob he used his .22 and shot a roo right in the head from about 40 metres, killing it instantly. I was impressed with the skill and accuracy he possessed with a firearm. Nick was not as impressed, and proclaimed he could do the same thing. He was letting his competitiveness get the better of him. "Good luck, mate," scoffed Shepard as he handed the rifle to Nick.

"Don't worry about me. Us Tazzies are pro with the gun," Nick replied.

We drove for 45 minutes without seeing any animals for Nick to back up his claim. The night's cold temperature was taking away the pleasure of being outside. Shining the light in between a small group of trees, we finally saw the eyes of another animal looking back at us. We drove closer along the scrub line and saw that it was a large kangaroo standing alone about 30 metres from the truck. "Let's see if Nick can put his money where his mouth is," Ades whispered to me, not wanting to spook the roo.

Nick lined up his shot, pulled the trigger, and hit the roo square in the temple! The shot didn't seem to do anything but disorient it for a second before it slowly hopped away from our location. The bullet must have ricocheted off of its skull. "Shit," Nick cursed. Looking for redemption he fired a second time and once again hit it in the head, but to our amazement the roo just shook it off and continued to hop away. The third shot hit it directly in the face, blowing some of the animal's jaw away and sending teeth and fur flying. But it still remained alive. Its bulging eyes and shattered teeth reflecting back at us from the spotlight made my stomach turn. Four shots later, the roo still clung to life. It lay crumpled into a ball on the ground, breathing heavily with its face barely recognizable.

"C'mon Nick, that's enough. Put the fucking thing out of its misery," I shouted.

"I'm trying to, but the bastard just won't die," Nick yelled back at me.

"You are a terrible shot, Nick," Shepard said as he leapt out of the box of the truck. Reaching behind the backseat he retrieved the police baton, walked over to the suffering animal, and in one swing caved in the roo's skull to end the nightmare it was in.

That experience ended any motivation we had left to hunt. With that we called it a night and returned to Shepard's house. The drive home was silent as we each reflected on the events that had unfolded during the course of the night. That ended up being the first and last time I ever hunted in Australia. The four of us never spoke of that hunting trip again.

Chapter 8

One Tree Wonders

I can't recall what sort of project work I had been doing that Thursday, January 22nd, but I can safely say that I was struggling to keep my productivity at a high level. Victoria was experiencing a heat wave that consisted of temperatures peaking in the high 30s, and I was still in the process of acclimatizing to my new work environment.

After the work day had finished, I started the 20-minute walk home to begin my usual routine of making dinner and enjoying a cold beer. Just as I got to my front door, my cell rang. Seeing it was the Depot calling, I answered with my usual work greeting, "Harold here."

"Get to the Depot, mate. We got a fire for you," said Kev in his distinct muffled voice.

"I'll be right there!" I said, turning around and running back from where I had come.

Halfway back to the Depot I was picked up by one of the firefighters who had also received the call. We drove the rest of the way to the Depot in his truck. Once at the Depot, I went straight to my locker and immediately changed into my green firefighting uniform for the first time. Wearing the uniform gave me the sense that I was finally about to fight a fire, and this realization caused a familiar tingly sensation to flow through my blood.

There is a strange feeling that comes over a group of people when they know they are about to fight a fire. The mix of excitement and trepidation from the rookies coupled with the veterans' stoic faces creates a tension in the air that I cannot compare to any other situation. A dynamic bond is shared by the rookies looking for the veterans to give them strength, while in turn the veterans look at the rookies with a nostalgic amusement. This is a powerful but unseen force that is not always appreciated.

Grabbing my backpack from my locker, I laced up my work boots as others scurried around the Depot preparing themselves for the work ahead. "Where was the fire called in?" I asked Gogo as he passed me on the way out the shop door.

"Just a small smoke in the Black Range, mate. Maybe you'll pop your cherry today," he answered with a tailored cigarette hanging from his bottom lip.

Gathering around Kev, the six of us received a quick informal briefing about the fire situation. The smoke had been sighted by one of the neighbouring lookout towers and didn't appear to be getting any bigger. This smoke had most likely been caused by a hold-over fire that had started by a lightning strike and smoldered throughout the night only to start up again in the heat of the following day.

After Kevie's briefing, Gogo, Rags, Simon, and myself jumped into two of the Land Cruisers and followed the Tanker that was being manned by Ades and Beckett west towards the Black Range in hopes of finding the fire that had earlier revealed itself with the help from the sun.

As we navigated the winding dirt roads that cut a path through the thick forest, my adrenaline began to pump in anticipation of what a wildfire would look like in this country. After 30 minutes of traversing through the dirt roads of the Black Range we turned a sharp corner and saw the other two vehicles parked with our fellow firefighters peering down the slope.

"Looks like we're here," Ragsy commented to me while slowing our Land Cruiser to a halt. Getting out to join our crew, I looked down the hill only to have my adrenaline cease immediately. I saw that this fire was what we affectionately referred to as a "one tree wonder."

An area close to the roadside no larger than 50 square metres was covered in dark ash with no active flames on the surface. In the middle of the ash stood a five-metre tall broken eucalypt stump with flames licking its interior as they looked for a way out. It was clear that this fire had been started by lightning with how the top of the stump had been shattered and frayed by the enormous force that had been pushed through it. The chance of this fire escaping was minimal based on how little fire activity there was and considering that the daylight was already starting to disappear along with the heat of the day.

Before we could extinguish this fire, we decided to build a hand line around the burnt area in order to contain the fire in its current state. The handline wasn't exactly necessary due to how inactive the fire was; however, we decided to build one anyway. The hand line, made by manpower and without heavy machinery, is essentially when all of the unburnt vegetation is pulled away from the fire's edge to create a bare area that the fire cannot burn into. The width of the hand line is usually less than a metre and can be as long as several kilometres. The distance the guard is constructed to the fire's edge depends on how actively the fire is burning. If the fire is burning hot, you would want to give yourself some space from the heat in order to save yourself from getting burnt.

An effective hand line is constructed by the whole crew accomplishing several tasks at once as a cohesive unit. The sawyer and the swamper are usually the first two firefighters in the line. The role of the sawyer is to cut any timber that is too large to be removed by hand and to fall any hazard trees. The swamper follows behind the sawyer and looks out for the sawyer's needs such as carrying the chainsaw fuel and their axe while also looking for any approaching hazards. The rest of the crew clears out the debris and shrubs that are left behind in the sawyer's wake. The goal of each firefighter with a rake-hoe is to not clear all of the vegetation in front of them but to take one swing with the rake then take a step, followed by rake, then step, and so on enabling everyone to participate in the hand line.

If the firefighters in the front of the line are removing all of the vegetation, this would leave little work for the rest of the crew at the back. If the line is moving too slowly and the firefighters in the back find they have nothing to do, then they simply have to yell "Step up!" indicating to the firefighters at the front of the line to bump ahead in order to leave work at the tail of the line. Usually the firefighters at the front will be removing heavier vegetation than at the back, so positions in the line can be changed around in order to manage fatigue

- especially during the times when the hand line can take several hours to construct.

The hand line around this small fire was easy to make with our rake-hoes and little digging was required to clear away the dead leaves that had fallen from the overhanging trees and the bracken (a fern-like shrub) which covered the hillside. It took us no longer than ten minutes to complete the two-foot wide hand line.

During the hand line construction, Ades brought out the 660 chainsaw and opened up the stump to expose the burning embers hiding inside the smoldering husk. His chainsaw work made it easier for the rest of us to scrape away the charred wood from the rest of the stump, separating the burnt fuel from the unburnt.

One of the plastic yellow hoses was then pulled from the tanker and brought down to the smouldering remains that had just been gutted from the stump. Once the water pumps were turned on, we soaked down any heat that was still trying to fight for survival. The wood hissed and steamed as the water poured out of the nozzle and onto the targets. It did not take much water for the fire to be extinguished, but we emptied the water tank on the whole area for the extra insurance and peace of mind that the fire was out.

After running our bare hands over the surface of the extinguished stump and not feeling any heat - a process also known as cold training - we were satisfied the fire was out and began the demob of our gear.

From start to finish we were not on the fire for more than an hour before we headed back to the Depot to share some after fire beverages and to toast our first Aussie fire of the season.

Only two days after my first Aussie fire I received my second fire call on that Saturday afternoon while I was at home on standby. We were not required to work on the weekends, but when the fire hazard was high we had the option of being available for work at a reduced wage while we hung out at home. Only two rules applied while on standby: we had to be within 30 minutes of the Depot, and we could not have any alcohol. This made it a boring weekend for some of the guys.

Pep had received the same fire call, so he picked me up in his truck and drove me to the Depot to get ready for the fire that lay ahead of us. Pep was a couple of years older than me and loved being a family man to his wife and three girls. He was one of the smallest guys at the Depot, but had a personality as large as Australia itself. He was the Depot jokester that kept the work atmosphere light but would frequently cross the line into inappropriate humour that would make some of the older fellas cringe. Several times a week during the morning briefings he would hug the first person he saw and not let go until awkwardness would set in, forcing the other man to pry Pep away. I enjoyed his company and I was stoked that I was about to fight a fire with him.

Once we arrived at the Depot we received our marching orders from Kev to head south into the Blue Range and meet up with the Marysville crew to locate a smoke that had been called in by one of the lookout towers. Marysville is the town south of Alexandra, and due to their close proximity the two districts would join up and fight fires on a regular basis.

While Pep and I loaded up our assigned slip-on, I inquired about bringing a couple of wajax bags: portable rubber back-packs that could be filled up with water attached to a hand hump and nozzle.

"What the hell would we do with that?" Pep asked while he stuffed his fire gear into one of the side compartments.

"To put water on the fire."

"We never use those things. They've been collecting dust on the shelf for years, mate. Besides, we have water in our tanks if we need any," he said as he closed the side compartment on the slip-on.

"Back home that is one of the main tools we use, and they are super effective. Never go to a fire without them," I tried to reason.

He laughed as he jumped into the driver's seat. "Let's go, you crazy Canadian. The fire's not going to wait on us."

Along with another six firefighters in three slip-ons, we traveled about half an hour until we met up with the Marysville crew at the designated area in the Blue Range. The Marysville crew of six was led by an older, burly man by the name of Curls, due to the long hair he had once possessed in his youth.

The fire was not visible from the side of the road but was located a couple hundred metres somewhere up on the hillside from where we had parked. The lookout tower could no longer see the smoke, so we would have to grid the area in order to find this fire that was now concealed by the forest. Usually we wouldn't go into a forested area with an unseen fire, but the weather was cool, we wouldn't be too far from our slip-ons, and with the lookout not being able to see smoke we felt safe enough to travel into the bush unsecured from an anchor point.

The twelve of us lined up 15 feet apart along the roadside and began our ascent up the hillside. The forest was full of mature trees and tall bracken, making the rolling hills difficult to scout the area at any distance. As we marched up the hills, rake-hoes in hand, I looked at the bright green uniforms walking in unison and was reminded again of how alien this was for me. Not only was I looking for the smoke that would reveal the fire's location, but I was also looking for any poisonous critters that the other firefighters had become accustomed to living with. My caution shifted my focus from the task at hand onto the environment that I was still learning about. I decided to trust the men beside me to give me a heads up if we encountered anything hazardous and to regain my focus back to searching for the fire.

"Got it!" came a yell from one of the Marysville firefighters to the right of me. "Just over the hill there." I couldn't see where he was pointing, but everyone on our side of the line turned towards his direction and started walking.

The fire was on the downward side of one of the curves in the hillside, which explained why it had been hidden from our view along the roadside. This fire was almost a duplicate of the fire I had just fought in regards to its size and origin. The fire was burning on the inside of a 20-metre tall eucalyptus tree that had been struck by lightning, most likely from the same thunderstorm that had started the last fire. An ash perimeter of 75 square metres surrounded the smoking tree with no visible smoke coming from anywhere but inside of the eucalypt.

Before we could commence the rake-hoe line we were instructed to wait two tree lengths away from the fire while one of the Marysville firefighters felled the smoking tree with the large chainsaw that he had packed in. The two tree length distance is a standard measurement used in both countries. This distance ensures that if the tree falls, lands on another tree, and causes the additional tree to fall, all firefighters will be clear from potential harm.

After hearing the tree crash to the ground from the sawyer's excellent work, we went back to the fire and continued the process of constructing the rake-hoe line and chopping up the fallen eucalyptus tree so we could remove the burnt fuel and crush up any of the smouldering embers and any other sources of heat. This extinguishment took a substantial amount of time compared to the last fire. Without having access to this fire with our slip-ons, we had to extinguish the fire completely without the aid of water. Dry mopping is the term used for putting out fire without water. Dry mopping is an effective and necessary strategy to use when there is no water available, but it is more time consuming than wet firefighting. I wanted to bring up with Pep how useful the wajax bags would have been in this situation, but I didn't feel like pressing the point. I was a guest here and I was willing to learn how they fought their fires in a country I had no experience in.

After Curls was satisfied that the fire had been extinguished, we returned to our slip-ons and drove back to our respective areas where we would once again celebrate another successful fire by having a few beers and some laughs at the Depot. We would only have to wait another week before the next fire started, a fire that would put our skills and experience to the test.

*The wildland firefighter recruits at the 2008
training camp in front of the Alexandra 2 tanker.*

*Instructors Craig and Phil with recruits Bob, Dash,
Josh, and Dok (Left to Right) at training camp.*

The Alexandra crew taking a break from the relentless heat while clearing the hiking trails of the Cathedrals.

Gogo bucking up a tree that is blocking one of the many roads that are maintained by the firefighters.

*Ragsy, Ades, myself, and Beckett (left to
right) after our first fire of the season.*

*The Alexandra and Marysville crews constructing a
hand-line around a smoldering eucalyptus tree.*

Firefighters hiking towards the fire's edge in Beachworth.

The smoke coming from the direction of Marysville on February 7th, which can be seen from the Alexandra Depot over 40 km away.

Me and Pep (left to right) before our descent into Marysville.

Fire on Martin Road as it approached Marysville.

*The last of the firefighters to escape off
of Kings Road in Marysville.*

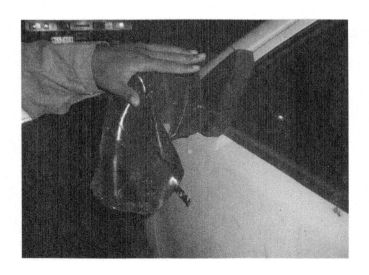

*The melted mirror of the truck that
Josh and I used in our retreat.*

*Firefighters and Marysville residents in the
Oval the morning after Black Saturday.*

*The destruction after the fire had passed
was difficult to comprehend.*

Mat and I spent weeks together working the night shifts.

*Mat and Em overlooking the Rubicon Forest
as it burned throughout the night.*

Chapter 9

Beechworth Fire

After the one tree wonders, the next week went by without a fire call. The wait to get back onto a fire was starting to weigh heavily on the crew. There is only so much equipment maintenance and make-work projects you can do before you start to yearn for the dynamic change of pace that a forest fire can provide. It's a strange balance of morality and duty that occupies a firefighter's mind when waiting for a fire call. Nobody wants to see property loss or have people put in danger; however, without the fires that occur we wouldn't have this job that becomes a part of our identity.

I have found that there are three motivating factors that influence firefighters to do this job that requires them to run towards fires when others are running away. Some do it for the excitement and the status that is perceived to come along with being a firefighter. Others do it out of a sense of responsibility to help those in need who can't help themselves. Then of course there is the money aspect of the job. Fires usually lead to long hours of overtime that result in extra cash in a short period of time.

As luck would have it, shortly after I arrived at work the following Monday morning I was dispatched to a fire close to the town of Beechworth, which is located 200 km north east of Alexandra. Once again I was paired up with Pep in one of the land cruisers while Gogo, Dash, Old Bob, and Laura manned up two additional slip-on trucks.

With Gogo in the lead truck, the rest of us followed him for three hours to our dispatch location at an old hospital that was no longer in use on the outskirts of the town. Upon arrival we found out that this rundown hospital would be our accommodations for the duration of our stay. We unloaded our bags into the old psychiatric ward. Each room had whitewashed bricked walls that contained two single cots, the type that are only a couple of inches thick with heavy springs holding the bottom together, as well as an old dresser and a chair. Aside from my initial surprise at where we were staying, no one else seemed to be shocked at all that we would be bunking up in an abandoned hospital. Any experienced firefighter has stayed in far worse conditions, and having a roof over your head is a luxury that should not be taken for granted.

After we had checked into our rooms, we gathered in the hospital parking lot where we met up with 12 other firefighters from that district. A local firefighter informed us that a Rappel crew, Wildland firefighters that could belay from ropes out of a hovering helicopter, had been working on the fire since the early morning and that the fire had grown bigger than they could control. The temperature was already in the mid 30°C range and we were told to expect the temperature to continue to be hot for the remainder of the day. We loaded into our trucks and followed the local crews out of town and into the forest where we would help support the firefighters already working on the fire.

As soon we arrived at the ridge top that would be our staging area for our vehicles, I could see light, white smoke mixed with bursts of light brown colour rising from several hundred metres down the hillside. This type of smoke indicated that although the fire was consuming vegetation slowly, it was not burning at a consistent rate. A thick column of continuous dark copper-coloured smoke would have told us that the fire was burning at a higher intensity and that an initial attack would not be possible. Thankfully for us, this was not the case.

While we were getting our gear ready for our assault, Gogo met up with another firefighter who had clearly been working the fire by the presence of black soot that covered his face and green uniform. When Gogo returned from his chat, he informed us that the fire was a couple of hectares in size and spreading slowly up the hillside. Dozers would be coming within the hour to establish a dozer guard around the topside of the fire, but the flanks were burning in an area too steep for the dozers to safely drive into. Our objective would be to construct a hand line on each flank of the fire in order to tie in with the dozer line to effectively box in the fire.

With our camelbacks full of water and tools in our hands, all 18 of us marched along the top of the ridge then down the slope towards the incoming smoke. Looking at the men and women beside me, I noticed how much older some of the firefighters were in comparison to who I had been used to working with back in Canada. Four of the men walking in the line beside me had to be in their late 50s or early 60s. Their wrinkled leather faces caused by exposure to decades of the strong Aussie sun hinted that they had put their bodies through a lifetime of manual labour. It wasn't worry that occupied my mind when working alongside these older gentlemen but more of a reverence for these firefighters who had devoted their lives to this job. Even though this was my ninth year fighting fire, in comparison to them I had just started. It made me wonder if I had it in me to do this job until my body couldn't physically do it anymore because of the limits that come with old age.

We walked straight down the slope. Once we reached the left flank of the fire, we immediately began to establish a hand line by raking a one-metre guard down to the mineral soil. The forest floor consisted of the usual sparse understory of bracken along with mass amounts of ground litter from the fallen eucalypt leaves. The ground was still flat enough for the dozers to work, but we did not want to leave any unsecured fire behind us.

The flames were one to two feet high and moving at a rate of one metre per minute. The fire was burning hot but not intense enough that we could not construct the hand line adjacent to the flame front. The flames here looked sharper and burned a brighter shade of yellow, and they were accompanied by a thicker, darker smoke than I was used to. The smoke from the burning oily vegetation caused my eyes to also burn and well up, a side effect which added to the difficulties of the workload.

We continued working on the hand line for 150 metres until the slope increased in steepness beyond what the dozers would be able to operate on. From that point about half of the crew, all members from the Beechworth district, went back up our newly constructed hand line and started to establish another hand line along the opposite flank.

Pep and I took up the rear of the line on the crew that continued down the left side of the fire. The steepness of the hill caused our group to slow down considerably with most of us having to hold onto trees or dig our rake-hoes into the ground for stability. Since Pep and I had taken up the rear of the line, we had to take extra care so as to not dislodge any rocks that could come rolling down on our fellow teammates below us. We also had to make sure that the line behind us was complete without any fire crossing our hand line.

After 15 minutes of intense hand line construction, we noticed that the gap between us and the front sawyer had become rather large, and after another 10 minutes we could only see two other firefighters on the line ahead of us. Several small fires which had spotted over the line behind us were causing us to ignore the hand line and extinguish these spot fires. Our best strategy was to pull the burning vegetation back into the other side of the guard. After a short period of time we had secured the line but noticed that we were the only people left working in our area.

"Those guys must have moved pretty far ahead, Pep," I told him as he struggled to catch his breath. Taking a drink from my camelback I took a moment for a quick breather and to collect my thoughts on the situation. Sweat now poured out of every pore in my body as I fought to hydrate myself. "What do you think?" I asked him.

"They'll be right, mate. If they need us they would give us a holler," he wheezed between breaths while he leaned on his rake-hoe for support. "Besides, someone has to take care of this shit up here."

"I'll be right back. I'm just going ahead a bit to see if I can locate the rest of the guys."

"No worries, mate. I'll be right here sucking air for a few anyways," he said while trying to smile at the same time. I continued down the line until the forest opened up to reveal the rest of the crew 300 metres down the hillside where the slope had leveled off to a flatter area. A clear hand line was constructed from me to them. Seeing that they were not in immediate need of our help, I hiked back up to Pep.

"Doesn't look like they need us. We should go back up our line and make sure no more spots have crossed over," I suggested, remembering how easily the fire had spotted over in the area that we had just held.

"This is bullshit. We take care of the hard part while those bastards stay down there," he said while wiping the sweat from his face.

Climbing back up the hill while staying on our hand line, we were relieved to find that no fires had spotted over. We made our way back to the area where our group had previously broken into two and found a constructed dozer line that ran along the hillside over towards the other flank of the fire. As we followed the dozer guard we ran into Gogo who was standing beside a drip torch and rolling a cigarette. He now resembled the firefighter he had talked to on the top of the ridge with a comparable amount of soot covering his face and uniform. He had been burning off any unburnt fuel between the fire's edge and the dozer guard in order to further secure the perimeter. "How was that for ya, Harry?" he asked after lighting up his smoke.

Before I could answer I had to take a few seconds to catch my breath from the climb up the steep section of our line. "Loving every minute of it," I managed to say.

"Probably a lot different than your pussy fires back in Canadia," Pep cut in from a short distance behind me. Gogo let out a short laugh and offered his pouch of tobacco so I could roll myself a cigarette.

"Thanks, Bud. How's the rest of the fire looking?" I asked Gogo while flashing my middle finger towards Pep, causing both of them to chuckle.

"Looks like we got the hard part licked, mate. Go for a walkabout and check it out. I'm going to continue down your side of the fire to see any other areas that need to be burnt off," Gogo replied.

Leaving Gogo to continue in the direction that we had just come from, Pep and I continued to walk along the dozer guard to the opposite flank of the fire. The dozer guard ended after 200 metres and tied into the far hand line that the other crew had established after we had parted ways an hour earlier. Flames that had once burned freely had now run into their hand line and been reduced to smoldering logs and debris.

Looking down this flank of the fire I noticed a familiar fire-fighter with a bright red bandana walking towards me. "Eben! How's it going?" I yelled over to my fellow Canadian. Eben and I had completed Alberta firefighting training together five years earlier, but we had never been on the same fire. Eben was working with the Rappel crew that was dispatched to this fire. Funny how it took us both going to the other side of the world for us to finally fight the same fire.

"Good to see you, Buddy. Working like your visa depends on it, I see," he responded with a grin. "I saw your boys on the other the side of the fire and they said I could find you up this way." Eben and I talked about the fire for a few minutes while we hydrated, then we parted ways to work with our crews for the remainder of the day.

We worked until the sun began to set, reinforcing the dozer guard and hand line by putting out any potential problem areas that could spot over in our absence throughout the night. The total fire size came close to five hectares by the time we were told to return to the hospital. A skeleton crew of firefighters would stay overnight to watch over the fire and make sure it remained contained inside the guard until the following dayshift would arrive. Exhausted and dirty, we left the fire and returned to our rooms in the psych ward to rest for the night.

Early the following morning we drove back to the fire and walked around the guard to make sure the fire hadn't escaped into the forest during the night. The hand line and dozer guard had done its job and held the fire to the same size as when we had left the night before. By now the fire behaviour had weakened to the point where visible flames were hard to spot. The remnants were only evident by the smoldering logs and dark ash where vegetation and debris had once stood. Without any available water sources we had to dry mop the entire fire, thereby making the extinguishment a slow process.

A species of tree called ironbark occupied a large part of the hillside that we worked on. The ironbark tree is just as the name suggests and is easily the hardest wood I have ever been exposed to during a fire. The sheer weight of this wood added to the workload when having to move or turn over these blackened skeletons. The larger logs required a considerable amount of chainsaw work to open them up in order to expose the burning coals. This added yet another challenge to putting this fire out.

Working long hours over the next two days, we continued to dry mop the fire. We worked from the perimeter of the guard and slowly towards the middle of the fire to eliminate any sources of heat. It was satisfying to fight this fire from the point of it being out of control, to containment, and then to full extinguishment.

Our last night at the hospital was spent in the old courtyard, sipping on beers that we had picked up from the local liquor store. The unused courtyard's tables and chairs were covered in a thick layer of dirt and leaves that we had to dust off before we could relax in them. It is always an exhilarating feeling to be sent to a fire, but on the other hand it is also a good feeling to be sent home. Knowing that we had done our job to the best of our abilities and the thought of sleeping in our own beds kept smiles on our faces as we unwound with our well-deserved beverages. The following morning we were released from Beechworth and drove back to our homes.

During the following three days the temperatures began to rise to an even more uncomfortable level than I had thought possible. With the nights being so hot and the days being even hotter, the threat of wildfires became more and more apparent as the days passed. Everywhere we went the grass was completely cured, their blades and stalks now brown and void of any green pigment. Dried vegetation cracked under our boots and blew away in the wind. The expectation to have us ready to be dispatched to a fire kept us close to the Depot for most of our working hours. It would have been cruel to send us out to do project work in the hot sun and then expect us to bust our ass fighting a fire after being exhausted by the heat.

Temperatures peaking in the low 40°C range became a daily unwelcome occurrence that I was having a hard time adjusting to. In my lifetime I had only felt a handful of days in the mid-30s, and while living in Northern Alberta for the previous four years the mercury had never cracked the 30°C mark. The nighttime lows stayed in the high 20s and low 30s, which did little to relive the relentless chore of trying to stay cool.

Over those three days that first week of February, 2009, the temperature rose over 43°C with the high never dropping below 28°C the nine days prior. This heat wave became a record-setting event for the hottest consecutive days in Victoria that still stands to this day.

We should have seen what was coming, but how could we have possibly known.

Chapter 10

Black Saturday, February 7, 2009

It was around 3:30 p.m. on February 7th, and I was drenched in my own sweat watching the cricket test match on the television. The extremely hot temperature was starting to take its toll on my body and all I could do was lie on the old brown couch and sip on water to battle the dehydration that constantly seemed to creep up on me. A weather update interrupted the match to announce that Melbourne had hit a new record temperature of 46.6°C with a relative humidity of only six percent. Almost on cue with my thought of how difficult it would be to fight a fire in these extreme conditions, my phone rang.

It was Kev. Fires had broken out across the State of Victoria and I was needed at the Depot as soon as possible. His distinct muffled voice was not as relaxed as it usually was when he had previously dispatched me to fires. The stress he was feeling was evident over the phone, giving me cause to worry about the fire I was going to. I grabbed my backpack, jumped on my bike, and raced the ten minutes to the Depot in the sweltering heat.

Upon arrival at the Depot gates, I once again looked south towards the massive smoke column coming from behind the rolling hills. The towering smoke had risen several hundred metres in the sky and was continuing to build upon itself like a giant grey and white castle. Back in Canada, smoke columns this extreme indicated how fast the fire was escalating with almost no chance for containment, which I had no doubt meant the same thing here. The winds were progressively increasing, causing the boughs of the eucalyptus and peppermint trees to sway back and forth. Dry sand constantly assaulted my face as it travelled on the steady gusts that blew throughout the yard.

Turning my attention back to the Depot, I could see several others hastily changing into their green uniforms while others continued to load up gear into the work trucks and our red tanker. "What's going on, Kev?" I asked as I got off my bike.

"Victoria's burning, mate. You're going to help in Marysville," replied Kev. His tan-coloured shirt had a dark ring of sweat below the neckline. Hearing the office phone ring, he turned back into his office to answer the incoming phone call.

Seeing that I wasn't going to get any more information from Kev, I went to my locker and changed into my greens. Due to the intense heat, myself as well as the majority of the other firefighters kept our green tops off while we completed our duties of getting all of our gear organized and ready to go. Rumours and speculation floated around the Depot as to what we would be doing, but no one seemed to have any concrete answers pertaining to the monumental task that lay before us.

All we knew was that earlier in the day, several of our firefighters had been dispatched to another fire that had started close to the Mirrindindi Mill. Kev had called in the remaining eight firefighters and six Vic foresters to go to the fire that was burning to the south of us. The crew that was previously dispatched to the other fire was comprised of most of our senior firefighters, which left a lot of the inexperienced rookies and foresters that I had gone through training camp with.

Jack, a tall, slender man with dark cropped hair in his early 30s, was going to be the person in charge of our crew. He was an experienced Vic forester who worked in the office up the hill, and until this point I had never worked with him.

Since it was the weekend and everyone was on standby, it took another half hour before the last person had made it to the Depot and was ready for deployment. In the meantime, I was paired up with Pep, my Zimbabwean friend Josh, and Chris, a second year firefighter, in one of the Hylux trucks. Once everyone was ready to go, the 14 of us loaded up into the three Hyluxs, three Land Cruiser slip-ons, and the tanker and we started the 41 km drive towards the giant smoke column that was rising from the direction of Marysville.

Every kilometre closer to Marysville the smoke column grew exponentially in size. As we followed the convoy we could see farmers packing up their families into their vehicles along with whatever valuables they deemed important. Other Emergency vehicles with their flashing lights screamed past us towards an unknown destination. Cars stuffed with people and their belongings passed us back towards the direction of Alexandra.

We pulled our trucks over to the side of the road before our final descent through the hills that led into the valley where the town was built. We gathered outside of our vehicles and stared in wonder at the power on display before us that was the cause for so much pandemonium on the roads and in the countryside. Looking up, there was a clear divide where the thick smoke was slowly closing out the blueness of the open sky. Even though it was only five p.m., the darkness was quickly approaching us with the help of the thick blanket of copper smoke that had begun to swallow the majority of the heavens.

Jack told us to wait while he and Sam drove into town to make a plan and see if it was safe for the rest of us to follow. Most of us lit up cigarettes in anticipation of what was going to happen next while the non-smokers wished they had started that habit to ease their nerves.

"So, what do you think?" Nick inquired as he stared at the wall of smoke in front of us.

"Man, I have no idea what the hell we are going to do about that," I replied, nodding my head in the direction of the smoke. "I doubt there's much we can do." My adrenaline was maxed out, surging the familiar tingly sensation throughout my body. The constant rumbling mixed with the wind the fire had created caused us to raise our voices just to hear one another. The strong winds made every tree branch and piece of vegetation wave towards Marysville as if the fire was beckoning us to face it head-on.

"There's no fucking way we're stopping that!" Pep interjected. I had to agree with my friend about his perspective on the incoming fire. Some felt the same as us while others just stood there and gawked at the force being unleashed in the valley.

Thirty minutes passed before Jack and Sam returned from their scouting mission. The decision was made that we were going to indeed fight this massive dark cloud that was climbing over the landscape. The fire hadn't reached Marysville yet, but it was only a matter of time. The plan was to meet up with the local DSE and CFA firefighters and stop the fire from burning into the town. Marysville was partially evacuated, but there were still residents who had stayed behind out of a willingness to defend their homes or had not received any warning to leave.

Putting our trust into Jack, we loaded back into our vehicles and started the journey into the smoky valley. As we drove closer into town, the smoke particles in the air increased with every passing second. Downed branches and entire trees were starting to accumulate on the road, due in part to the constant tugging by the wind caused from the fire. Our drivers had to slow down the pace in order to swerve around the hazards laying across the road. The odd car came speeding past us in the opposite direction, but not as many as I would have assumed with a population of 500. I hoped that most of the residents had already fled from their homes to find refuge in the homes of relatives or at a hotel in another town.

At 5:52 p.m., we reached the outskirts of Marysville and immediately noticed several vehicles labelled "State Emergency Service" stopped in the middle of a road that led to the north of town. The orange uniforms worn by the staff at the scene indicated that they were not part of the DSE or the CFA. Looking closely behind the emergency vehicles, I could see a car that had been crushed by a fallen tree which had landed across the driver and passenger doors. A man wearing no uniform was standing on the hood of the car frantically using a chainsaw to try and cut the fallen tree clear of the vehicle.

"What the hell?" Pep whispered to himself as we looked at the situation in front of us. My initial instinct was to get out and help these people, but I wasn't sure where my job duties were taking me. An unfamiliar voice came from our truck radio stating that a woman and child were caught in the vehicle but the situation was under control. No additional help would be required. With that our convoy of vehicles continued for another couple of minutes until we reached the heart of Marysville.

We drove through the town and up a steep hill onto Kings Road where the town limits met the forest's edge. There we met up with local DSE firefighters as well as two additional tankers: one from the DSE and one from the CFA.

Since the fire that was burning towards us on the other side of the hill would be too hot to directly attack, it was decided that the best chance of fighting this fire would be to light a back burn. This form of fighting fire with fire is a tactic that is used to burn off all of the vegetation between a control line and the main fire, with the control line here being Kings Road. With the enormous size of the fire on the other side of the hill, the back burn would hopefully be pulled towards the main fire as it sucked in the large amounts of oxygen it required to sustain itself. After lighting the back burn, our goal would be to extinguish any embers that could float across the road and into the residential area. This would all be done with no water and only our rake-hoes.

With the plan in place, we were instructed to spread out along Kings Road to prepare for the upcoming task. Everyone parked their vehicles back in the direction of town towards our safety zone, an Aussie rules football field that was approximately 800 metres away. All of the vehicles were spread out no more than 50 metres apart. We parked our truck with the two tankers at the end of the street where Kings Road intersected with Martin Road. This also happened to be the furthest point from the footie field.

While we spread out along the road, I took the time to survey the scene around me. The paved intersection of Kings Road and Martin Road met at a sharp "V" with the corner pointing south. The paved road then transitioned into dirt, heading into a dense old growth forest. From this corner everything from the south and east of the road was covered in thick vegetation with a continuous closed tree canopy.

On the other side of the road were several houses within 20 to 30 metres of the forest. The majority of the houses were two-storeys in nice condition with unfenced yards that consisted of short dry grass.

On the corner of Kings Road stood a large, square brown house with a burgundy front door and an aluminum roof. Besides the one large tree that grew in its front yard, the vegetation that surrounded the house was fairly thin and clean. The couple that lived in that house watched us from their front yard as we spread out along the road in front of them. The man was middle-aged and dressed for the hot weather in shorts and sandals. He seemed relaxed and paid us little attention as he sipped on his beer and attempted to water his dried out lawn with a garden hose that had water barely trickling out of the nozzle. His wife, whose swollen belly indicated that that she was very late into her pregnancy, stood behind her partner. She was obviously unaware of the giant fire that was obscured behind the forest in front of them. For all I knew, they might have thought that this was just another sunny Saturday afternoon.

"Why isn't anyone telling them to leave?" I asked Nick as he lined up to the right of me.

"They can stay if they want. Your house is your castle, right?" was his rationale for the couple that were clearly ill-equipped to defend their home from any type of fire. It was absurd that these people were here with us, but I felt it wasn't my place to be telling them what to do. In Canada, when a forest fire is encroaching on a community, it is standard practice to evacuate all of the residents. If they refuse to leave, then the police will kindly escort them out.

"Pep, what's the plan?" I asked Pep, who was lined up on my left. I wanted some assurance as to what would happen next.

"Watch this back burn and look after the houses behind us. If shit gets real we'll hear it on the radio," he replied, indicating to the radios in our truck.

"How the hell are we supposed to hear that when we're not in our trucks?" I questioned. Throughout the season I had been constantly annoyed that we were not issued hand-held radios, but no more so than at that moment.

"She'll be right, mate," he said before turning his focus towards one of the firefighters who was walking with a drip torch to the corner of the road. "Get ready, Haz. Show's about to start."

At 6:29 p.m., we stood on Kings Road with our rake-hoes in hand and watched as the firefighter started the back burn.

The mood in the air was light as we observed the mixture of diesel and gas that poured out of the drip torch to form a singular thin line of flames along the road's edge. The orange flames slowly gained in momentum as they started to walk across the ground and into the forest. The flames danced across the forest floor, increasing the crackling and hissing coming from the oily vegetation as it burned. As the line of fire met the trees, flames easily climbed up the dry flakey bark of the eucalypts to further the fire's momentum. The rate of spread from the back burn was amazingly fast. Less than five minutes after the back burn was lit, a 100 metre section of the forest was completely on fire. Entire trees from the stumps to the crowns were engulfed in bright yellow and crimson red fire. Instantly, any trace of daylight disappeared as the sky was blackened out by the thick smoke. Our world that we had perceived to be in control of had now changed.

The heat radiating from the fire made us retreat off of the road and into the front yards of the houses to seek some relief from the oppressive warmth. Glowing embers from the tree tops began to drift high over our heads and into the residential area behind us. Without instruction, each firefighter began to search for spot fires that may have ignited from the drifting sparks that multiplied with every passing second.

I went behind the brown house and found three small fires that had ignited in the dry leaves. With my trusty rake-hoe, I quickly pulled dirt over the flames to keep the spots from spreading, but as soon as I would put out one small fire, two more would take its place somewhere else in the backyard. At this point I started to realize that we were in a losing battle. We did not have the resources available to stop the fire in the current conditions. Knowing that I could not put out all the fires that were continuously starting around me, I went out towards Martin Road to look for any available firefighters who could help.

What I saw when I left the backyard I could not comprehend. At 6:43 p.m., I observed what looked as if another back burn had been lit five metres into the forest running north along Martin Road. The entirety of the forest was ablaze and burning so intensely I could only see a silhouette of an emergency response car and a couple of firefighters in front of the burning forest. I had absolutely no idea where all of this fire had come from. Was is possible another back burn had been lit without my knowledge? Had the main fire found its way to us? Without a radio or any other communication, I was completely in the dark as to what the hell was going on. I had lost my situational awareness and an unfamiliar feeling of fear began to grow within me.

The thick smoke was starting to become a cause for concern. I had worked in a lot of extremely smoky situations, and I was always able to maintain my oxygen intake without too much stress. The smoke here was different, almost more oily, and it was making it hard for me to breathe, even when it appeared I wasn't surrounded by heavy smoke. The fear that had crept into me was now very real, and for the first time in my firefighting career I had no control as to what was happening around me. Not only were my lungs starting to struggle for breath, but my eyes were starting to become affected from the smoke as well. They were welling up and beginning to tear up so badly I was having a hard time seeing. This loss in vision only added to my stress. What the hell had I gotten myself into?

Taking a moment to compose myself, I knew I had to start preparing for the worst. I threw on my goggles and soaked my bandana with water from my water bottle, tying it around my face to cover my mouth and nostrils in an attempt to alleviate the debilitating effects of the dense smoke.

Moving to the backyard of the brown house I saw Pep walking towards me. Countless embers floated in the air like fireflies, each one illuminated in the dark smoke. Fires were now burning the bigger vegetation in the backyard and smoke was coming from the back deck of the brown house.

"This doesn't look good, man!" I yelled to Pep over the noise of the fire. The smoke was so thick I was having a hard time speaking as it filled my lungs with each breath.

"Yeah, mate, we need to get the fuck out of here!" he shouted back. We started to run towards the left side of the brown house that was our closest route back to our trucks. As soon as we had come around from the back of the house the forest seemed to explode. The heat was so intense we had to scramble back behind the house for shelter from the intense heat.

"Other way, Pep!" I yelled as we darted to the other side of the house to go around the opposite corner. Instead of seeing all of our firetrucks and the crew, I only saw two trucks, a couple of other firefighters, and a burning inferno.

Everyone else had fled.

Chapter 11
Trapped in Marysville

Everyone must have either acted on their instinct to get the hell away from the fire that was burning out of control or they had gotten the order to make a tactical retreat back to the safety zone. Their reasons for leaving didn't matter now, and the few of us that remained needed to escape! With no vegetation left to ignite, the fire had spread to the fences and houses that bordered the forest. Dark smoke filled the air, causing the day to appear as night. The light from the fire burned brighter in the absence of the sun.

As Pep and I ran out from behind the brown house that was now covered in embers and smoke, one of the two remaining trucks drove in front of us, acting as a shield from the heat coming from the wall of flames on the other side of the road. Behind that truck, Pep and I could see our Hylux abandoned on the other side of the road. The radiant heat had ignited all four of its tires, looking as if the Ghost Rider had commandeered our vehicle. Wordlessly we both knew that our truck was no longer an option for escape.

Pep opened up the back door of the truck in front of us and stuffed himself in the already crowded back seat. Seeing that there was no physical way I could fit back there with the others, I flung open the front passenger door, planning to jump onto the forester's lap who was sitting in that seat.

As I started to climb into the truck, the steering wheel was in my way! The forester pushed me back with one hand and looked at me as if I was an alien. In my haste I had forgotten that in Australia the driver sat on the right side of the vehicle.

"Sorry man," I apologized after I realized that both of us were not going to fit in the seat. "You guys go. I'll be fine." I am not sure why I just didn't run to the other side of the vehicle.

"You sure?" the driver asked.

"Yeah, go for it," I reassured. With that, he drove off and quickly disappeared into the black smoke.

As I looked for another way to escape, the strong winds that swirled in all directions threw burning debris and embers all around me. I was alone. Even the couple that was previously standing outside of their brown house had disappeared. I hoped for their sake that they had choose to flee and had not attempted to find safety in their house. I had to make a decision fast. This would be a decision that would either save my life or end it in a way I did not want to imagine.

Only several moments had passed when suddenly Josh, the forester from Zimbabwe, appeared out of the smoke from the direction of Martin Road. His bloodshot eyes and heavy breathing indicated he was having a difficult time in the smoke. Temporary relief came over me from knowing I wasn't alone, but that reprieve soon disappeared when I remembered that this was the first fire Josh had fought and that this country was as foreign to him as it was to me.

"Haz, what do we do?" he asked, looking for an answer that I was still trying to find in my head. The fire had completely surrounded us, reducing our visibility to no more than 15 metres. Trying to make it to the safety of the footie oval on foot was not an option. The chance of losing our way in the dense smoke or being caught in a part of the fire that we couldn't see was too high of a risk.

"The truck!" I yelled, and pointed at the one hope of escape I could find. Without another word we both started running towards the burning vehicle. But after running only a few feet towards the truck I turned back because of how powerful the heat was. It felt as if my skin was going to burst into flames, and I didn't think we could make it without suffering severe burns or having our lungs seared shut from breathing in the scorching air. Without being able to retrieve our only source of escape, my first instinct was to run into the brown house and lay down in the bathtub with the shower turned on. Sticking to the only rational decision I could think of, I started to sprint towards the only protection I could see.

As I approached the burgundy front door of the brown house, I heard the wheels of a vehicle skidding to a stop on the road behind me. It was Josh! He had braved the unbearable heat and rescued our truck from the flames. The once flaming tires were now only smoking, with the short drive having extinguished the burning rubber.

Turning around to my salvation, I ran towards the truck at a speed I didn't know I was capable of. My mind couldn't process how fast my legs were moving, and before I knew it my momentum had carried me hard into the rear driver's side door, throwing me back onto the ground. Reaching up I grabbed the door handle to pull myself up. Black plastic smeared into the palm of my glove from the soft rubber of the melting door handle. After throwing myself into the truck I slammed the door behind me. "Go!" I yelled to Josh, not realizing that he was already driving forward. My adrenaline was pumping so hard that all I could hear was my heartbeat thumping in my eardrums.

Black smoke immediately engulfed our truck. "Can you see anything? Can you see where we are going?" I shouted. I couldn't tell if Josh had answered me because of the deafening ringing in my ears. Josh stoically held his hands on the steering wheel and continued to drive forward. As we pressed on through the darkness, hoping to stay on the road, I could not see more than a couple of feet in any direction. The headlights did little to aid us with their beams of light fading only several inches from the hood. Ash blew through the only remnants of light in front of our truck that strangely reminded me of driving in a snowstorm. After a couple minutes of crawling along the road, Josh brought the truck to a halt.

"Why are we stopped?" I asked. I leaned forward in an attempt to see through the smoke and made out a large tree that had fallen across the road, blocking us from our escape. The girth of the tree was too thick to drive across. We couldn't risk getting out of the truck to cut the tree off of the road, as we knew we would have suffocated from the smoke. We were trapped! Our only option was to stay inside the truck and hope that the fire would pass without burning us alive.

Burning embers smashed into the windows, exploding like tiny fireworks as each one met the glass. Sparks slowly began to come out of the air vents and into our truck. Josh quickly turned off the vents to try and keep the sparks at bay, but it did nothing to change our world that was crumbling around us. The fire was starting to find its way to us, and there was nothing we could do about it. As the temperature in the truck began to rise, I came to the sobering realization that I was going to die. I knew in my heart that the fire was going to somehow find its way inside of the truck and consume us both. I imagined the last thing I would see would be the windows shattering and flames rushing in. In that instant I missed my family. The thought of them hearing that I would never be coming back to Canada tore up my insides.

I was in the one situation all firefighters think they will never be a part of: a situation where all control was lost. All of the events that day had led up to this one moment that was beyond my comprehension. The only certainty in my mind was that this is how it all ends. I was going to burn to death.

"Josh, we fucked up. We fucked up," I kept repeating. I grabbed three water bottles from the truck floor and poured them all over my head and chest, attempting to relieve myself from the heat. I turned around to get the fire blankets out from behind my seat, anticipating that they would give us the extra protection we were in need of. Right as I was ripping the plastic cover off of the blankets, Josh yelled, "Look out!" At that instant a tanker truck belonging to the CFA came rushing by us and slammed into the fallen tree, pushing it to the side. There was hope.

Our avenue of escape had once again been opened up and we no longer had to wait to see what fate had in store for us. We drove forward and smashed through the broken limbs of the fallen tree that had tried to keep us from leaving. Josh pulled up close behind the CFA tanker, using its flashing red lights as a guide which was making it easier to stay on the road. Behind us, another tanker caught up to our truck and began to closely follow us. The tankers, which must have been around the corner of Martin Road, had made the decision to retreat after us.

As we crept through the blackness, both tankers turned on their sprinklers to shower us in heavenly water. I let out a deep breath and along with it all of my fears. An overwhelming feeling of relief swept over me knowing that we were going to make it. The tightness in my chest relaxed and I was able to breathe somewhat normally. "We're going to be fine," I assured Josh as well as myself. Josh didn't say a word. The only hint I had that he was more at ease was that his death grip seemed to have loosened on the steering wheel. Thirty-five minutes had passed since the back burn had been lit.

After what seemed like a long time, we broke through the smoke and I could see the footie field only 100 metres down the road. Even though we were no longer caught in the thick smoke, the blackened out sky made it hard to see the field in its entirety. Multiple work trucks, tankers, and civilian vehicles along with several firefighters and residents were spread throughout the turfed field. A flashing display of emergency lights lit up the safety zone. Silhouettes of burning buildings and torching trees outlined the perimeter of the oval.

Without being in need of the escort from the tankers, the one behind drove ahead. This allowed us to follow at our own pace. Josh turned around to me for the first time since we had gotten into our truck and smiled. The whites of his eyes were completely red with small burn marks on his cheeks from defying the heat and retrieving our truck several minutes earlier. "We made it," he breathed.

Looking at the oval green field, I replied, "Yeah, Buddy. I didn't think we ha-" BOOM! An explosion came from the back of our truck, causing us to duck down in our seats. Lifting my head to look through the rear window I saw the entire back of our truck was covered in bright flames. My adrenaline surged again as I got out of the truck and began throwing burning backpacks and objects as far away from our truck as possible.

Looking up, I saw a truck with a slip-on racing beside the fire's edge towards us. As the truck got closer I could see Jack and Sam. They had left the safety of the field and come back for us! When Sam skidded the truck to a stop beside us, Jack jumped out and started the small pump on the slip-on. He pulled the hose over to our truck and began to spray down any remaining flames that lingered on our truck.

"You guys okay?" he asked.

"Yeah, thanks. I think so, now," I replied.

"Was there anyone else behind you?" he inquired while he moved his attention from the truck to the burning bags on the ground around us.

"It was hard to tell. I lost track of where everyone was," I answered truthfully. After looking at the charred backpacks and seeing they couldn't be salvaged, Jack turned off the pump and spooled up the hose. We got back into our trucks and drove down the rest of the hill to join our crew in the safety of the short green turf.

Getting out of our truck, several of the Alexandra firefighters rushed towards us to see what had happened. "Holy Shit. Look at your truck!" Nick said excitedly, pointing to the passenger side of our truck. The black outside edge of the mirror now draped downwards in a hanging glob which resembled the melted clocks in Salvador Dali's painting, *The Persistence of*

Memory. The truck's white paint was speckled with black spots and brown burn marks from our escape. Looking in the back of the truck, I could only see the remnants of the burning equipment and bags that I had tossed out up the road.

"Where's my bag?" asked Chris. His usual curly red hair now lay damp and matted across his forehead.

"Something exploded in the back of the truck. Had to ditch them up the road," I replied.

"Ah shit," Chris sighed, "That was probably my aerosol deodorant. Sorry, mate."

Looking at my fellow firefighters, I could see by their blood-shot eyes and clammy, red skin that they had also been exposed to the fire. Most of them seemed in good spirits with smiles on their faces. The joy of living was hard to contain after coming so close to never making it off of Kings Road. For a lot of the firefighters in the oval this was their first big fire that they had been a part of and they would still have to come to terms what had just occurred and what was still to come.

Pep informed me that all of our firefighters were accounted for and that none of them were hurt. I was relieved finding out that no one I knew had been caught in the fire.

Grey flakes of ash continuously rained down as I surveyed the scene around us. The dark sky was illuminated with dark orange and crimson red hues from the trees and houses that were being consumed. The silhouettes of the large trees that bordered the circular field looked eerie against the burning backdrop of houses completely engulfed in flames. The loudness of the strong winds and the roaring of the fire sounded as if a plane engine was running beside my head.

There was an equal amount of residents to firefighters that huddled in the field for refuge. They talked amongst themselves and wandered around with looks of confusion or resentment as to how their lives had just tragically changed. One woman sobbed into her husband's arms as he tried to console her grief. An older man lay very still on a grey blanket as a man and woman knelt beside him and tended to his burns and laboured breathing. A local artist sat in a car, covered in a blanket with an oxygen mask attached to his face. The back of the car was stuffed full of paintings he had deemed important enough to save from his burning home before he had fled for safety.

Needing to collect my thoughts, I sat down beside Dok who was using the wheel of a truck to lean his back on. The usual happiness that radiated from his blue eyes was now replaced with a deep sadness. "Do you think anyone died?" Dok asked. He repeatedly ran his fingers over his long golden beard, perhaps out of nervousness or in an attempt to groom it free of ash.

"It's hard to imagine that everyone made it out," I answered, trying to be as sensitive as possible. For some unknown reason I kept the truth from Dok that there had still been people in the houses behind us when Josh and I had left Kings Road. We stared hopelessly at the destruction for several minutes until a medium-sized dog ran past us, looking for comfort in the wet grass provided by the tanker sprinklers. The scared dog had large patches of fur that that had been burnt off and replaced with charred flesh. Looking back at Dok, I answered him honestly this time, "For sure a couple of people didn't make it."

Most of the other firefighters believed that everyone had made it out of the fire. We all survived, so why wouldn't everyone else? Denial is a very powerful weapon against a reality that you don't want to be a part of.

Most of the tankers kept their flashing lights on in an attempt to guide anyone who may still be stuck in the wake of the fire.

A couple more residents would appear in the field after we arrived, but not many. Without knowing who had fled before the fire and who had decided to stay and try to protect their home, it was impossible to know who had made it out and who had not been so fortunate. I continually scanned the field for the couple that I had seen at the brown house but they never appeared.

The fires had knocked out the town's electrical power. Not only did this disrupt the town's hydro, but it also disabled the cellular tower. This prevented any reception to our cell phones. There were rumours that other towns had been burnt over, but these rumours could neither be confirmed nor denied from the outside world. It must have been hard for the people I worked with who couldn't reassure their families that they were safe. As far as their families and friends knew, we had gone to fight a fire and hadn't returned. I wondered if Bonnie had any idea where I was or if she knew what was happening around her home. She had left for vacation that morning, and we hadn't talked since her departure from the airport.

For hours, the fire stayed at the same intensity, slowly burning everything around us. We sat in the howling wind and watched as the trees and shrubs would torch up. One by one, buildings would catch on fire and slowly be devoured by flames. I heard house windows shatter and observed the fire pouring out of the new openings it had created until the house would eventually crumble in on itself. Throughout the night, loud explosions erupted around us caused by exploding fuel tanks.

Every possible escape from the town was blocked off and no one dared to leave. There was nothing any of us could do but wait.

Chapter 12

The Aftermath

Hours passed and no one slept as we watched the flames burn out and turn into the smoking remnants of what had previously stood around us. The black sky highlighted with fire eventually faded to solid grey and when the daylight appeared around seven a.m., the enormity of the destruction was difficult to comprehend. The majority of the houses around the field were now gone; in their place only red brick chimneys surrounded by unrecognizable charred debris remained. Trees that were pushed over from the gale force winds enhanced the post-apocalyptic background.

A handful of the houses remained intact and unburnt but were no doubt affected by the smoke that had filled each one. I was reminded of the Kelowna fire of 2003, when the fire would devour certain houses but leave others as if it had a particular taste for how to please its appetite.

By now, most of the people who had taken shelter in the field were standing together talking about the night's events.

Overall I would guess that there were around 60 people that had spent the night waiting for their escape. The town residents mixed in with the green and yellow uniforms of the firefighters amongst the firetrucks and cars that were covered in a layer of grey ash. Folding tables had been set up and covered with first aid supplies and drinking water for whoever was in need. I could overhear whispered rumours about friends and neighbours who had not left town but were still unaccounted for.

Even though the active fire had subsided over the night, we were still unable to leave the field. The massive amount of trees that had fallen onto the roads would have to be removed before we could utilize them once again. Several firefighters took their trucks and began the task of clearing a path out of Marysville.

While we waited for our exit to be cut, we continued to converse with each other, sharing our stories of escape. I joined a conversation between an older gentleman wearing a CFA uniform and one of the Vic Foresters. The older man was explaining how thick the smoke had been while he was trying to drive his tanker to the field last night and that at one point he had barely missed ramming into one of our trucks on Kings Road.

"I was in that truck," I interrupted.

"Oh, sorry mate. I couldn't see much with all that smoke," he said apologetically.

"No worries. If it wasn't for you we would still be stuck behind that tree."

"What tree?" he asked, all confused. In his escape, he hadn't even noticed that he had pushed aside the tree that was blocking the road when he had passed by us. Josh and I thanked him and assured that there was no need to apologize for almost rear-ending us. In fact, he had most likely saved the both of us.

After thanking him again, a small helicopter appeared in the sky and briefly hovered overhead before landing in a clear spot on the side of the field. A NEWS woman and a cameraman exited the helicopter and began to conduct interviews with some of the local survivors. After a short while, the NEWS crew boarded the aircraft to find another story or to return to where they had come from and report what they had found. I was left confused as to why they had not taken any of the wounded with them to the nearest hospital.

At 11:04 a.m., after 16 hours of restless waiting in the footie field, we finally got the order to load up into our trucks and convoy out of what was left of Marysville. The air remained heavy with smoke as we departed for our homes in Alexandra. Driving slowly out of town, my heart sunk further seeing that the destruction wasn't contained to the area we had just spent the night in. Almost every building in Marysville had been burnt to the ground. Metal signs, brick walls and chimneys, collapsed tin roofs, and cement pillars were the only evidence that remained. The smoking charred foundations of each building resembled black skeletons with nothing left to salvage. Burnt vehicles were scattered throughout the town and on the sides of the roads, most of them melted down to their metal frames. Their numbers grew with every passing moment as we drove further out of town. No one in our car spoke as we surveyed the damage.

The amount of trees that had fallen on the road slowed our pace as we weaved between each broken piece. Occasionally we would pass a vehicle that had been caught in the fire, each one with its insides and tires eviscerated which left only a black metal shell. As we swerved around a blackened motorcycle that lay on its side in the middle of the road, I wondered what had happened to its driver. I hoped that whoever it was had found somewhere safe to hold up until the fire had passed.

Most of the farms and ranches on the outskirts of the town had suffered the same fate. Their houses, barns, and other farming infrastructure had all been reduced to piles of ash and smoldering debris.

Cattle and other livestock lay dead in the ditches and throughout the paddocks along the road. The carcasses that were not completely burnt had their stomach fully bloated with their tongues hanging out of their mouths in the dirt. Each face was frozen in a distorted gruesome pose of their last moment alive.

Halfway to Alexandra, the burnt edge of the fire was finally behind us; however, the smoke continued like a fog that never lifted. Even as we arrived back to the Depot around noon, the smoke remained thick in the air.

Kev was waiting for us at the picnic table outside of his office. The puffiness of his squinty eyes suggested he hadn't slept during the night. He cared for each of us as if we were his own family and I couldn't imagine the worry that had gripped him knowing where he had sent us the previous day. No one had to tell Kev about what had happened for him to understand what we had been through. He had lived through the Ash Wednesday fires in 1983, and knew firsthand how devastating a fire could be.

The fatigue from the night's events along with 30 hours without sleep showed on every firefighter. Kev could see by the looks on our faces that the only thing we wanted to do was retreat into the shelter of our homes. He instructed us to take the rest of the day off and to return the following afternoon to begin working the night shift.

Exhaustion hit me like a tidal wave when I finally accepted that the day was over. I didn't even take the time to change out of my green uniform before I left the Depot. Being distracted by my inner thoughts of trying to process the night's events, I forgot about my bike and began to walk home.

My cell phone now had reception for the first time since the fires had taken out the cell service, and it continuously buzzed with incoming texts from coworkers and friends who I hadn't seen or heard from since I had left for Marysville. Bonnie, who was on vacation on the West Coast of Australia, had seen the fires on the news and had a hard time containing her concern and sentiment over text messaging. I thought that she must have assumed the worst when I read the text from her telling me that she loved me. That would be the first and only time she would say those words to me. I sent her a text back explaining what had happened and that I was okay, but no reply came. I wouldn't hear from her for another couple of days until after she had returned from her holiday.

Passing through downtown, I noticed that Alexandra was far busier with people than usual. Seeing those people with fear in their hearts, I then knew that this fire was not just another fire. This was an event that would forever change the people who were involved. This fire would be remembered for the loss and heartache it would cause for an insurmountable amount of people.

A lady seeing me in my firefighting uniform stopped me to ask if Alexandra was safe from danger. After nodding yes with my eyes half closed and letting her know that she was in no immediate danger, I dragged my heavy feet the rest of the way up the street.

I found my house empty when I returned home. Both of my roommates had families that they needed to take care of and I had no idea as to their whereabouts. Stripping out of my greens, I grabbed a cold beer from the fridge and made my way to the TV. All five channels were showing the fires that were burning throughout Victoria in some form of news media. Quickly I found out that Marysville was not the main source of news as far as the media was concerned. Hundreds of fires had been reported to have started and several other towns and communities had been burnt down or affected by the fires in one way or another. The town of Kinglake had been completely destroyed and was the focal point for the majority of the debates and interviews. It seemed that every few minutes a live report would confirm another casualty of the fires by flashing a smiling picture of a person who would never be seen again by their families and friends.

I knew it wouldn't be long before the news travelled back to my home in Canada, and so I phoned my parents to let them know I was okay and that I missed them. I continued to phone other family members and close friends, seeking some level of comfort. Most of them had no clue that there were massive fires burning on the other side of the globe. As much as I could hear their support over the phone, I could tell they were a world away with how little my news seemed to affect them. One of my friends even told me that she was too busy to talk. I had been fighting fires my whole adult life and so hearing about my job was nothing new to them. But I knew that this was somehow different; it seemed more real, more personal. I had never been on a fire where such a loss was felt. I had just gone through an experience that I still did not comprehend, and it was difficult for me to convey that over the phone.

I sat on the couch and continued to stare at the TV. So many people's lives would never be the same. The images and stories of tragedy became more and more powerful, as did my fatigue. Realizing how close I had come to never seeing the people I cared about again, I was overcome with emotion. I lit a cigarette, put my head in my hands, and shed the type of tears that only come with someone who has nothing left emotionally.

That was the loneliest time of my life.

Chapter 13

Rubicon

The morning after Black Saturday, I awoke to the lingering smell of the burning forest. Looking out my window, I could see that the air was still saturated with grey smoke as if no time had passed since I had fallen asleep. The vast amount of smoke that was being produced from the fires made it hard to tell how far away the fires actually were. Smoke from large fires have been known to cross oceans so I couldn't use the greyish haze as any type of indicator. It was difficult to think of anything aside from the fires that were still burning. Every TV channel and radio broadcast was still focused on the tragic events that had happened on that unforgettable night.

After a late breakfast, I began to get my gear together for the upcoming night shift. We were tasked to work at night for several reasons, the most important being that the fire behaviour would be significantly reduced due to the drop in temperature and the decrease in the wind. Heat exhaustion was also a real threat when working in +40°C temperatures, and the difference of 15°C would be hugely beneficial.

Another reason we worked the graveyard shift was that it was hard to recruit enough volunteers - who made up the large majority of Victoria's workforce - to fight fires throughout the night. As much respect as I have for the men and women who sacrifice their time to help, I understand how hard it would be to work away from their homes and families for free while putting their lives at risk.

Although the fire's nighttime behaviour would increase our safety from the flames, firefighting in the dark came with additional dangers that were not always present during the day. Working at night in an area that was unknown, which for me was pretty much everywhere, restricted visibility. This of course made driving and following directions that much more difficult. The increase in certain hazards because of the reduced visibility made directly attacking a fire challenging to do at a reasonably safe level. Instead, the man-power would be allocated for structure protection, to reinforce areas where the fire could escape, to create dozer lines and fuel breaks, and to provide reconnaissance for the upcoming day crews.

I wasn't exactly sure what my approaching nightshift would entail, so I packed enough food to last me 24 hours as well as some warmer clothing. Working nightshifts back in Alberta was rare and I had only experienced it a handful of times. Even during the summers in Alberta, the nighttime temperatures drop to a point where the fires will not actively spread, and since we had to camp on the fireline and not get paid for it, overnighting on fires had become somewhat non-existent.

I was tired of sitting in my house alone with only my thoughts to keep me company, so I headed to the Depot to see if I could be of any help before my shift started at six p.m.

Walking up the Depot driveway, I noticed that it was strangely quiet. Usually a handful of firefighters would be scattered around the property tinkering with some sort of fire equipment, but the only person I could see was Kev. The dark circles under his eyes hinted that he hadn't slept since I had seen him the night before.

"What are you doing here?" he asked. "You don't start for a couple more hours. Go home, mate."

"I don't have anywhere else to go," I replied. With that, he nodded his head and forced a small smile on his tired looking face. We sat on the picnic table out front of his office as he filled me in on the whereabouts of the rest of the crew. Everyone was either gone from the Depot fighting a fire or would be arriving in the next couple of hours to join the night shift. He had no idea how many fires were currently burning nor of how many there had been. All he knew was that everywhere around Alexandra was on fire and we would be working non-stop for the foreseeable future.

"Since you're here you might as well be useful and help prep the trucks," said Kev. As we were walking through the door that led into the warehouse, I noticed a large silk strand of a spider's web dangling across the doorway. Instantly, I jerked my body backwards and bumped into Kev, avoiding the web and not pissing off any poisonous spider that had created it.

"What the hell are you doing?" Kev asked.

"A web," I explained.

"What web?"

I looked back at the doorway, only to see that the web was no longer there. I have thought about that moment a lot and have come to the realization that there was no cobweb. I was so physically and mentally drained that for some unknown reason I had reacted to a figment of my imagination. Kev just looked at me with his squinty eyes, shook his head, and walked through the doorway.

Over the next couple of hours, my fellow co-workers showed up to the Depot ready for whatever the night would have in store for them. Most of them greeted me with a tired "hello" as they yawned and tried to rub the fatigue out of their eyes. Each firefighter stopped by the whiteboard to see where they would be headed for the night. Kev would have most of us split up and go to different areas to help the massive volunteer workforce that had come to provide aid in this time of need.

My partner for the night would be Mattie Kav, a friend of mine who worked for Vic Forests. Mattie was a little over six feet tall with unkempt dark hair and a matching dark beard. He was always cracking jokes and finding the lighter side of life with his intelligent humour. Every one of his stories would end with him saying "you know what I mean?" with an open mouthed smile while he looked around for a laugh or reassurance that we understood his point of view. I had met Mat when I first moved to Alexandra through my roommate Dane at a barbeque. From time to time, I would hang out with Mat and our mutual friend Mick while they had impressive jam sessions on their guitars. They were both very gifted musicians, and so hanging out with them was always entertaining. Mat had been with my crew on Black Saturday, and I found it oddly comforting that I would be working alongside someone who had also experienced that night.

We were tasked to drive one of our Land Cruiser slip-ons approximately 15 km southeast to the Rubicon State Forest. This wooded area of century-old trees was located in the hills up from the Goulburn River. There we would meet up with Gogo, who would be our Operations Leader for the duration of the shift. Our goal would be to assist Gogo and a group of New South Wales (NSW) volunteer firefighters in a back-burn operation. We would conduct this back-burn off of a dozer line that had been constructed during the day in order to protect historical assets such as an old post office, power stations, and lumber mills that had been built in the 1920s and 30s. The fire that was burning throughout this forest was heavily situated on the southern side of the historical areas.

Before we could drive out of the Alexandra town limits, we had to pass through a road-block manned by the State Police. This road-block was to ensure that any non-essential people wouldn't be travelling to areas where the uncontrolled fire was still a threat, which at that point was pretty much everywhere. With a quick wave from the two policemen standing outside of their cruisers, we continued on to our destination.

The road leading up through the hills into this densely forested area was narrow and curvy like most of the forest roads in this region. Driving off of the pavement and onto gravel, we passed the historical post office. This old wooden building was surrounded by large trees and moderate-sized shrubs, making it a potential nightmare to protect if the fire found its way to it. "Let's hope we don't have to deal with that," said Mat as we continued up the road to our rally point.

As we got higher up the road, the daylight slowly fading into night allowed us to see the orange glow of the fire's edge on the distant hillsides. As we approached the flank of the fire, we followed a right hand curve in the road where we found Gogo standing beside his slip-on and rolling a cigarette.

"Good evening, gentlemen," he said while lifting his half-rolled drummie to his mouth so he could lick the glue. "Welcome to the Rubicon."

Behind Gogo, both sides of the road were on fire. To the right of us, the fire had burnt to the road's edge and continued to burn slowly down the slope to our left. Fire during the nighttime was strangely mesmerizing. Countless embers floated in the air as if they were coming from the clouds. With this amount of embers, it was no surprise the fire had spotted across the small gravel road. Inside the fire's edge, downed trees and shrubs burned. This burning was giving off an orange and yellow brilliance and helping us see into the darkened forest. Crimson flames danced around the bases of the ash and stringy bark trees, constantly throwing out embers that caused the fire to spread faster than it normally would. The tops of these giant trees disappeared into the blackness above us. Occasionally, fire would find its way up the trunks by consuming the loose bark from the ground to the crown and giving us a glimpse of the canopy overhead. The crackling of the burning wood was as constant as the slight breeze that flowed through the hills.

Gogo had previously patrolled the area and informed us that an old mill and a power station were the closest assets under threat and that they would need our attention sooner rather than later. A vast amount of fire perimeter was burning throughout the Rubicon and would also have to be patrolled during the night.

The three of us would be the only DSE firefighters who would be working in this area along with the NSW volunteer firefighters. Mat and I lit up cigarettes and discussed with Gogo the strategies and tactics that we would use in order to complete our upcoming back burn. For such an aggressive firefighter, Gogo was equally safety-orientated. He knew that my fire experience in this type of terrain was limited, so he made sure to be thorough in the safety briefing he gave Mat and I.

The cooler nighttime temperatures along with the higher elevation in the hills made the fire intensity low enough for us to not worry about being caught in the fire. The main danger that this forest presented was the high potential for the larger trees to fall down. As time would pass during a fire, the base of the trees or their root systems would sometimes get burned out, hence increasing their likelihood to fall. These dangerous trees are what we like to call "snags" or "widow makers". It was even worse in the old ash forests that had been burnt in years past. With no leaves and few branches left on the dead trees, they fell in silence until they crashed into the ground and then rocketed down the slopes like oversized white spears taking out anything in their path. If you were unlucky enough to be in the way of one of these falling giants, the chance of survival would be minimal.

Abandoned mineshafts were also a real threat in the dark. This area had been home to a rather large gold rush when Victoria was first settled by Europeans. During my project work it was commonplace to stumble upon an old mineshaft that led straight into the depths of the earth.

One by one, the NSW tankers came around the bend with their flashing emergency lights on and stopped behind our two slip-ons. The men and women unloaded out of their five tankers and rallied together in preparation for a briefing. Gogo and a man who was in charge of the NSW volunteers huddled around a map that was spread out on the hood of Gogo's Land

Cruiser. They discussed the plan ahead of us, and once they had decided on their strategy, Gogo raised his hand and spoke loudly to get everyone's attention. After explaining the hazards to the newcomers, he continued to describe in detail our task of burning off the vegetation from the dozer line that had been established around the values at risk. The fire was threatening the structures and we would be needed right away.

Right before Gogo could finish up the briefing, he was interrupted by a loud crash coming from down the hill. A hefty tree had fallen over and smashed onto the forest floor. Gasps and concerned mumbles came from the NSW firefighters. As the tree settled onto the ground, the abrupt noise was replaced by the never ending crackle of the fiery forest around us.

"Now that's why we don't work in the black at night," Gogo said trying to make light of the situation and reassure everyone's confidence. Immediately, I concluded it was bad luck to have a tree fall close to us and that having our briefing not directly beside the fire's edge would have been better for the volunteers' nerves.

We loaded back into our vehicles and followed Gogo through the darkness towards our goal. After a short drive, the forest gave way to an open area with sparse shrubs and lesser vegetation. A dozer line was constructed along the forest's edge creating a fuel break from the smaller shrubs and grasses. Gogo then instructed us over the radio to park our vehicles and group up so we could be positioned along the dozer line for the upcoming back burn.

As Mat parked our slip-on, I watched one of the NSW volunteers get out of his tanker and walk over to Gogo. After a brief discussion between the two, the man got back into his tanker, turned the tanker around, and drove off in the direction we had just come from. The other four tankers followed suit and retreated back down the hill.

Driving up beside Gogo, we got out to investigate the change in plans. "Where are they going?" Mat asked.

Reaching for his tobacco pouch, Gogo let out a long sigh and then lifted his gaze to meet ours. "They're going home, mate."

"What the hell do you mean, they're going home?" I asked in disbelief.

Gogo pulled out loose strands of tobacco and skillfully pinched little bits into his rolling paper. "They felt it was unsafe, so they went home. A small tree fell over and hit the side of one of their tankers. 'Fraid a tree was going to fall on their heads." As Mat and I took a second to let our new situation set in, Gogo lit up his cigarette and drew in a long breath of smoke. Exhaling a wispy cloud of smoke into the cold night air, he crinkled up his forehead while staring at the burning cherry at the end of his cigarette. "Fuck 'em. Looks like it's up to us."

Our man-power had suddenly been cut from several dozen firefighters and a fleet of tankers to just the three of us in our two slip-ons. Without the help from the NSW volunteers we would not have the resources that we would require to safely complete the back burn. The risk of the back burn jumping the guard was far too high and with only our two slip-ons, it would be too much for us to handle if the fire escaped. With every other firefighter in the State of Victoria working somewhere on a fire, we would not be able to get replacements for the man-power that had just left. We were in charge of this area, an undetermined amount of burning edge, and we still needed to protect the values at risk. We had to come up with a plan to best utilize our three-man army. "Righto, let's meet up with the dozers and see what needs to be done," Gogo instructed.

We jumped back into our vehicles and drove to a nearby mill where a dozer was working. This mill appeared to have been built during the turn of the century when they used to haul logs with horses. The mill site consisted of a small wooden rectangular building with a giant circular saw beside it. It hadn't been used in years but served as a reminder of how hard life must have been when the area was first harvested.

The dozer was in the process of completing the second dozer blade pass down to mineral soil between the mill and the forest. An ominous glow coming from deep inside the forest showed us that a more substantial dozer guard would be needed if we hoped to save this historic building. We also needed to figure out the extent of the fire's edge and determine how far it had moved from the previous reports. It was decided that Mat would stay with the dozer and help protect this area. Gogo and I would each take a slip-on in opposite directions to scout the fire's edge and get a better understanding of what was going on around us.

Gogo wanted me to go check the fire perimeter on the far side of the Rubicon. In order for me to gather this information I would have to drive back to our original meeting spot and continue up the road through an active section of the fire. He said that he had driven through it earlier that night and to be mindful of falling trees that may block the road. He added that some of the trees had already fallen onto the road, but these could be either driven over or around to reach my destination.

"Careful, you two. I'll radio when I get to the other side," I said before I drove back to our meeting area.

Arriving at the fire's edge, I stopped the slip-on and got out into the cool night air to better survey what was ahead. Both sides of the road were still on fire with the majority of the flames concentrated in the heavier vegetation that had yet to be consumed. A thick array of bright embers filled the air as flames lapped at the base of every tree that lined the roadside. With the drop in temperature and the slight increase in relative humidity during the course of the night, the heat would be manageable if I had to get out of my truck for any reason.

With the dark, the smoke, and the windy road, I couldn't see more than 75 metres in any desired direction. The road was cut into the steep hillside deep enough so that the bank on the right hand side was one or two metres higher than the roof of my Land Cruiser. The left hand side dropped off at a sharp enough angle that if I were to drive off of the road, I would roll to the bottom of the hillside 200 metres below. After factoring in all the risks associated with driving up this secondary road and putting my trust in Gogo, I decided that it was safe enough to try it out.

Driving beyond the first couple of corners, the forest seemed to open up with an eerie orange glow. The safety of the unburned forest behind me was now replaced with smoke and burning timber. Fire clung to life in whatever vegetation hadn't been burnt in the fire's initial pass. Now fully surrounded by the radiance of the fire, I could finally see how tall the towering trees were. *Please, for the love of God, don't let one of those trees fall on me*, I kept repeating in my head. I white-knuckled the steering wheel, hoping that my death grip would somehow make this drive safer.

As I came around a tight corner I was suddenly faced with a thick eucalypt tree that had fallen over the road. Luckily, it had fallen from the top side of the bank and was situated in a way that I was able to drive underneath it.

More and more trees appeared on and across the road. I had come this far and I would not be turning around now.

The next barrier was a smaller ash tree that had fallen perpendicular to the road. The girth of the trunk only stood a foot off of the ground, so I threw the Land Cruiser into 4L and stubbornly crawled over the wanna-be roadblock.

I drove over or around several other trees until I reached a large enough one that halted the drive. *Here we go again*, I thought, being reminded of the night in Marysville. This time I wouldn't have the luxury of a tanker blasting though this tree. It was time to use my snigging skills that I had obtained through hours of road clearing on those project days.

Turning around on the tight road, I backed the truck within two metres of the fallen giant and got out of the truck. The warmth of the fire felt nice on my face in the chilliness of the night. The smoke that surrounded me was more tolerable than I had anticipated. The oily vegetation had already been consumed by fire. Only the larger woody debris and tree trunks were burning, making the smoke somewhat manageable to work in. I grabbed the heavy snig chain and wrapped one end around the base of a tree trunk and the other end to my truck. I pulled my truck forward and victoriously moved the obstructive tree out of the way. Success!

After several more minutes of driving, the orange glow that lit up the forest faded as I made it past the fire's edge. Bright stars forming unfamiliar constellations appeared in the sky as I left the fire behind me. With my heart rate returning to normal, I relaxed my grip on the steering wheel and patrolled the unburnt forest on the far side of the Rubicon. As instructed,

I checked out several areas where there was infrastructure and figured out that the fire was far enough away that it wouldn't require our immediate attention. Relaying this information to Gogo over the truck radio, I was then instructed to go back to the old mill and meet up with Mat. Gogo informed me that he would be working with two dozers somewhere along the river's edge trying to put a guard around a spot fire.

Going back through the fiery passage that I had driven through an hour before didn't take as much time as the first pass; however, my heart was racing just the same. Thankfully, this time there were no trees that needed to be removed from the road.

When I arrived back at the old mill, I found Mat standing on the road puffing on a cigarette. The dozer he was working with had cleared the area around the mill and was slowly building guard along the ridgeline. The auburn highlights coming from the forest were more concentrated than before, telling us that the fire had moved closer to us. We were satisfied with the guard the dozer had created. The only thing left for us to do was to wait for the fire to come to the guard and then protect the mill from any impending spot fires.

"This is so intense. You know what I mean?" Mat said breaking the silence.

"Yeah man, I know. Have you been watching the NEWS? Messed up what happened the other night."

"I heard like 50 people died in Marysville," Mat said as he stared into the forest.

I felt the blood drain from my face after hearing the number 50. "That many? I'm still finding it hard to believe we were there and couldn't do a damn thing. What happened back there?"

Mat turned his head to look at me. "It was just too fast, mate. There was nothing we could do. It was like..." Mat opened his eyes wide and feigned a scream, "You know what I mean." Mat then took out another cigarette and lit it using the burning end of his current cigarette.

We sat on the slip-on and watched as the fire slowly consumed the vegetation up to the fire break. The guard did its job and we had to do little in regards to putting out embers or spot fires. The wind was in our favour and helped to minimize any fire brands from leaping onto the mill or across the guard. After the fire was no longer a threat to the mill, we spent the rest of the night patrolling the Rubicon and monitoring the fire's progress.

Before we left back for the Depot, Gogo met up with us to debrief the night's events. He had been able to contain the spot fire with the dozers and was happy with the work the three of us had accomplished with the limited resources we had. Standing in the morning light that came with the dawn, we could only laugh at the events that had unfolded during the shift and hope for a better tomorrow.

The following night I was assigned back to structure protection in the Rubicon. Once again I was paired up with Mat while Gogo and Emily would work together. Em worked for Vic Forests, matching the current theme of firefighter and forester working together. She was a tiny woman with glasses and brown hair that curled into tight locks. Em and Mat were dating, and I enjoyed hanging out with them.

In addition to Em, Gogo had requested support from paid firefighters in hopes of avoiding the "tactical withdrawal" that had happened the night before. Instead of the NSW volunteers, we got five tankers and a squad of firefighters from the NSW Parks and Forests, the equivalent to the DSE in Victoria.

Fires still raged throughout the Rubicon along the roads and into the unseen forest. The day crews had constructed firebreaks and completed back burns to help minimize the fire damage in the area. During the course of the day, the fire had crept close to another historic mill. Directly beside this mill, the ridge gave way to a steep slope that travelled several hundred metres to a road below. This slope, which had been cleared of all trees and shrubs, was once used for moving large harvested timber down the hill with the use of cables. Now this slope housed an open culvert that moved water from the top of the slope to a power station located at the entrance to the Rubicon.

We strategically spread out our man-power around several structures and once again waited for the fire to burn towards us. Most of us waited by the mill and watched the fires burn along the dozer lines below. Embers and sparks continuously spewed in the air, like giant Roman candles.

While standing back from the edge of the ridge, the fire generated a giant yellow backdrop surrounded by darkness that created perfect silhouettes of the firefighters looking down the slope before them. I could easily make out the outlines of Mat and Em as they talked to each other on the ridgeline. I snapped a quick picture of the couple and wondered what it would be like to work beside someone that I truly cared about.

The dozer guards and back burns did their jobs and held the fires in check that night. This time our support did not leave, a fact which was greatly appreciated and which alleviated some of the stress that was still felt from the night before. With the extra help we were able to leave the NSW firefighters on structure support while we patrolled the Rubicon.

We spent the rest of the morning hours on the lookout by a hydro station while we waited for our relief from the day crews. The dawn was always my favourite time of the night shift. Right as my blood would begin to feel thick from the fatigue that flowed through me, the warmth of the morning sun mixed with the calls from the kookaburras always gave me a second wind. I could finally relax knowing that my shift was almost done.

Overall, our efforts during those two nights had successful results. We saved dozens of structures and only lost two old trestle bridges. More importantly than saving structures, this time no one got hurt.

Chapter 14

The Grinding Blur

The three weeks of working the night shift after the Rubicon became a blur in my memory. Sleep deprivation mixed with the routine of patrols and working beside dozers seemed like one long shift. From working four nights in a row and then only getting two days off to "recover", I became more of a zombie than a firefighter. The excessive noise from the overcrowded town and the relentless heat during the day made sleeping almost impossible, and so most of the time I would go to work feeling more tired than when I came home.

Every day I would get up at four p.m. after my restless, broken sleep and put on my green uniform that I had previously discarded beside my bed. I would then drag my feet to the footie oval in town that was now being used as an evacuation centre.

Due to Alexandra being one of the few communities in the immediate area that wasn't directly affected by the fires and was relatively safe, a massive influx of people had relocated there for help. The oval was now the hub for anyone seeking assistance as well as the staging area for the non-local firefighters who had come to help. Rows and rows of white canvas tents were set up on the turf to shelter those who had lost their homes or who couldn't risk going back. First aid and relief tents were also set up for those in need. Two trailers were stocked full of donated items such as baby supplies and toiletries, and these items were generously given out to whoever asked. Dozens of volunteers moved around the oval like ants helping wherever their skill sets would best be utilized. The charity and selflessness of the volunteers that came to the aid of their community and their neighbours still warms my soul.

Before our shift, the Alexandra firefighters would unofficially meet at the mess hall by the entrance of the oval and have dinner together. It was our chance to meet up and check on each other. Sometimes you needed an understanding ear to help let go of some of the bullshit tension that can develop over a frustrating shift.

After dinner I would walk to the Depot, find Mat, and then check the whiteboard to see where we would be working for the night. To be honest, I have a hard time recalling much that happened over those three weeks. Most of the fires that had started on Black Saturday had burnt together, creating thousands of hectares of burning forest and countryside. It was difficult to know the extent of the damage or even where the fires had started or ended. Usually the work consisted of driving around and assessing the progress of the fire or helping with some variation of structure protection. A couple of times we attempted back burns, but the relative humidity was always too high at night for the burns to be successful. Protecting pine tree plantations with help from the dozers always seemed to be a popular assignment for Mat and I. I was just a grunt, so I was never part of any real decision-making. My job was to follow orders to the best of my abilities.

I once asked Mat how we were supposed to fight a fire on such a large scale. "Well, mate, how do you eat an elephant?" he said: "One bite at a time."

When I questioned the guys I worked with about what they remembered about the night shifts, I always got the same answer along the lines of "hard to remember" or "driving around in the dark". Gretch told me that he couldn't recall a single thing after the first days of the fire.

Each morning after we would end our shift at six a.m., we would crack a beer and trade some witty banter with the day shift crews as they arrived at the Depot. As we would walk to the oval for breakfast, without fail someone would stop and thank us for our hard work and tell us to be careful. We were easily recognizable to the public by our green uniforms and ash-covered faces. The heartfelt gratitude from these strangers helped to boost our morale and give the extra motivation we needed to keep going to work every day. I had fought fires in other areas where the residents hold onto the hate in their hearts after losing their homes. That persistence of blame and resentment makes the work environment a difficult place to be in, and I was grateful I didn't have to face that again.

My house was always empty when I arrived home, since both of my roommates would already be at work. I admit it was lonely. I had to stop watching TV, because it only ever showed stories or interviews of people whose lives had been destroyed. Every so often another casualty report would air and the total number of deaths would rise again. 23, 56, 78, 101... With chaos on such a large scale it was hard for information to be accurately collected and passed along. It was better to not think about it; that way I could keep myself functioning and go to work every day.

After almost four weeks of working nights, I got the welcome change of being assigned to the day shift. It was refreshing to sleep during the night and not have to avoid the sun like a vampire. That morning I looked in the mirror for what seemed to be the first time in weeks, and I saw a scruffy, exhausted version of myself that hadn't shaved since before the fires had started. The hair on my chin that was normally brown was now snow white. The colour change remained permanent and I wondered if all men's facial hair whitened this fast, or if it was caused from the stress of the never ending fires.

Arriving at the Depot for my first day shift in what seemed like forever, I was assigned to work with Ades and sent to the Big River State forest located east of the Rubicon. We were tasked to drive to a radio tower high up in the mountains and be lookouts for a couple of repairmen who needed to work up there. The fires were now somewhat controlled, but with the continued warm temperatures and no rain, the likelihood that a fire could get rolling again was still high. If we did notice a fire start to burn out of control, we would escort the repairmen to safety.

To get to this radio tower we had to drive up the dreaded Eildon-Jamison Road. This gravel road that started next to the highway and crawled its way up through the hills was easily the windiest road in Australia. You couldn't drive more than a couple of seconds before you hit a tight curve or switchback. We must have drove around several hundred corners in the hour it took to get to the tower. The unrealistic speed limit of 80 km made it more of a rally car track than a road for the general public. To add to the complexity of the drive, the road was littered with other fire vehicles or public cars that had permission to go back to their properties for the day to check on their houses and retrieve their valuables. This type of terrain was very different than in Alberta where I could drive several hours on flat country without making a single turn. Thankfully, Ades was an experienced driver, a fact which helped to keep my blood pressure at a reasonable level.

Once we arrived at the radio tower our day became less interesting. We did not have any choice but to stay on this mountain top and look for any approaching fire danger; however, the spectacular vantage point from where we sat made up for the boredom. Although most of the forest around us was unburnt, the active part of the fire in this area had long since passed and the chances of a flare up or spot over were low. Two of us were not needed, but due to the work safe policy we were not allowed to work alone. I didn't mind, though; it was nice to have the company. I had a chance to catch up with Ades, who I hadn't seen since before all the craziness began. He told me a riveting story about Black Saturday when him, Gogo, and Gretch were on the crew that went to a place where one of the fires originated close to the Murrindindi Mill. They had also experienced an intense day and were able to save a handful of houses that would have otherwise been lost without their efforts.

At the end of the shift, the repairmen informed us that they would need more time to complete their maintenance, and so for another day and a half we resumed our roles as lookouts without ever having to report any impending fire danger.

Once Ades and I were done with the lookout assignment, we were allocated to work with some of the American Firefighters who had come over to lend a hand. The Americans that came were all qualified in some sort of overhead position, and they had been asked to help manage the massive workforce that was going on the line every day. Our local crews were beginning to get burned out from fatigue and the extra help was very much appreciated.

Most of the Americans that I worked with were older and had a fair bit of experience under their belts. I forget what state they were from, but they were all in good spirits and enjoyable to work with. Ades and I gave them the tour of the area and introduced them to the crews.

One of the Americans I started a conversation with offered me a pinch of his chewing tobacco. After I accepted his offer and told him what a treat it was since chewing tobacco wasn't sold in Australia, he gave me the rest of the tin. Some of my Aussie buddies liked to talk about how much "harder" they were than Canadians, mostly to get a laugh or to start some debate on country superiority. After I got the tin of chew, I offered them a dip to see how "hard" they really were. Ades, Pep, and Nick all stepped up to the plate and put a pinch of the chew between their bottom lip and gum as instructed. I may or may not have told them that you need to spit out the excess saliva that builds up. After several seconds of them sucking and swallowing the chewing tobacco, they began to gag and spit out the chew while cussing about how awful the stuff was. Suckers!

Besides working with the Americans, I also got to spend a day working with a crew from Tasmania. Before this, my only exposure to the Aussies that lived on the small island to the south was Nick. My workmates were always giving Nick a hard time about being a bogan Tazzie. If the small-town Alex boys were calling other people bogans, I could only imagine how redneck the Tazzies really were. Unfortunately, the one Tasmanian firefighter that I was paired up with fit the fore-warned stereotype. He was a middle-aged man with a huge potbelly and a scraggly beard. His overbearing, vulgar, and racist jokes that only he laughed at dominated the majority of our time together. Spending most of my working career in the bush, I can appreciate a dirty joke or two – but there are limits. He was a nice enough guy but he had to be the crudest person I have ever had the pleasure to spend an afternoon with. He was a complete shitpump, meaning that everything that came out of his mouth was crap. Good thing Nick was a better representative for his island than that guy. I did however get to take a large Tasmanian Parks sticker that displayed a snarling Tasmanian devil with a wide open mouth full of teeth as a keepsake of our wonderful time together. I brought that sticker back to Canada where it found a permanent home on my guitar case.

On one of my last shifts I was paired up with Old Bob. This 40-plus year veteran was the oldest firefighter in Alexandra and for that matter, probably Australia. I had to give him credit for doing the job, especially initial attack, for as long as he did. There is no way I am going to be humping up and down hills on the fire line when I'm in my 60s.

We were tasked to go out to Lake Eildon and help support the construction of a "strategic fire break" in case the fire took another run towards that community. This fire break was pretty much just a massive dozer guard that cut through the forest in front of the town. Lake Eildon was a beautiful area to visit and it attracted visitors from all over the State. The lake's intrinsic value was just as important to protect as the expensive houses and resorts that were built along the shoreline and throughout the adjacent forests.

The drive out to the lake with Old Bob was pretty quiet. He drove and didn't like to talk much, at least not to me. After leaving Alexandra, he turned off of the main road and onto one of the slower sections of secondary roads. Shortly after, a mob of kangaroos appeared beside us bounding on pace with our truck. This is Australia! For some unknown reason, the largest of the roos that was leading the others decided that it would be a good idea to jump out of the ditch and land right in front of our truck. Before I could warn Old Bob, the poor animal had smashed head first into the bull bar and its lifeless body was flung to the side of the road. Straight faced Old Bob didn't flinch or speak, he just kept driving.

"Um, should we stop?" I asked after a few more moments of silence.

"Why?" he said in a tone that suggested a statement rather than a question. I only had to spend a couple of days with Old Bob to know what a trooper he was.

Sometimes it felt as if the fire had made me a prisoner to Alexandra. All of the roads going in and out of the town were blocked off by policemen and the only way across was on work business. One night while I was at the Commercial pub, I got a surprise visit that lifted my morale. Bonnie, in her green uniform and white truck, was able to drive through the roadblocks after giving the impression she was on work duty. It was the first time I had seen her in weeks, and it was uplifting to see my friend who had risked so much to come see me.

As the hours turn into days and the days turn into weeks, one's sense of reality solely revolves around the fire. As the routine sets in of work, eat, sleep, rinse, and repeat, you tend to forget about the other aspects of life that once seemed important. Even the money you are making becomes an afterthought to the seemingly never-ending mission set before you. With the enormity of a fire like this, the conclusion appears to be a dim pinhole of light at the end of the long tunnel – a light sometimes so faint that you need to forget about the end goal and just focus on finding your way through the darkness.

As much as most firefighters love their job, it is only human to miss the other aspects of life. Working day in and day out becomes a grind that each firefighter deals with in their own way. Most push away their thoughts of their personal lives in order to stay focused on the job. Your crew becomes your family as you deal with the stress and fatigue of the tasks set before you. The firefighters that allow their focus to shift towards home always find it challenging to deal with the grind.

It is usually not until you have come out from the other side of the tunnel that you realize that the rest of the world has continued on while yours has been stopped by the crimson beast of fire.

Chapter 15

Relief

The morning forecast on March 11th came with more than a glimmer of hope. Rain was on its way. That was hard for me to believe, because I hadn't seen any rain since before my arrival in Alexandra. Several millimetres of this forgotten water source was predicted to fall from the sky. After three months without any precipitation, the thought of something that could help break the drought was enough to lift everyone's spirits. Most of the fires that had once burned throughout the State were now under control or at least had fire breaks placed around their perimeters. A little bit of rain would give us the final punch that was needed to knock out these fires that had taken over our lives for the last 32 days.

Walking from my house to the Depot I noticed a slight difference in temperature compared to my usual morning walk to work. The air was a touch cooler, with a humid breeze that held the recognizable damp smell of an incoming rain shower.

After checking the whiteboard at the Depot, I was paired up with Dash and given a resident escort assignment. Residents that had been forced to leave were now allowed to go back to their homes to see the extent of any damage or to retrieve their valuables if they were fortunate enough to still have a house. With the fires still active, any resident who wanted to go back to see their property needed a firefighting escort, which that day happened to be Dash and me.

This particular assignment needed us to escort a couple from Alexandra to their home in Enoch Point so that they could check on their house and take whatever they felt was necessary. The small community of Enoch Point had once been a bustling gold mining town but now consisted of a handful of summer cottages. This beautiful area is nestled in the mountains beside a small river that once held the gold that sustained the thousands of people that lived there. The valleys and mountains that surrounded the town had been burnt, but as luck would have it, the fire did not make it to this community.

Usually on an escort assignment we would let the home owners take their time and do what they needed to do, but since the rain was coming the location of Enoch Point presented itself with some unique challenges. Their house was located at the bottom of the gully where the only road going in and out was a steep clay surface. If it were to rain while we were in the gully, getting back up the slick clay roads would be impossible. Once these red clay roads become wet, you might as well be driving on ice. Worst case scenario: the roads could wash out from the erosion that can occur after a fire and we would have to abandon our vehicle and hike out. That would not be how we wanted to spend our afternoon. To avoid this, we would closely monitor the weather and if we suspected rain was about to fall, we would leave immediately and come back to Alexandra.

Dash and I left the Depot and met the people we would be escorting at the eastern roadblock heading out of town. They were a pleasant middle-aged couple who drove an older blue station wagon that had no business driving on any surface apart from paved roads. We briefed them on the current situation and reinforced the fact that we needed to avoid the rain at all costs. After Dash let the policemen who were manning the roadblock know that the couple was with us, we drove through the blockade with the blue station wagon following behind us.

Driving through the hills towards Enoch Point, the sky was a darker shade of blue with the odd cloud starting to form. The windy road leading down to the river below was a red clay track cut into the hillside that was comprised of several sharp turns and switchbacks. Once we arrived at their cottage, we encouraged them to be as fast as possible and that an hour was the maximum allotted time we would give them to retrieve whatever they needed to get. We let them know that we would give them some privacy and that we would be patrolling the area. If they needed any assistance or they finished before the hour was up, they were instructed to give us a call on Dash's cell.

As we drove around the empty summer community that had been evacuated more than a month earlier, I could see why people would want to build a summer getaway in this isolated mountain retreat with the pristine river that carved its route through town. After we finished our patrol, we parked next to the river while we waited for the only residents in town to finish their business. Random bird calls and the rush of the flowing water were the only sounds in the absence of human activity. For that moment I was actually able to forget about the fires and pretend that I was enjoying a typical summer's day.

Dash and I talked about everything that had happened on Black Saturday and reviewed the different types of jobs we had been doing from then until now. Although I hadn't worked with Dash since the Beechworth fire, the work he had been assigned sounded familiar to what I had been doing. He had been working closely with the dozers creating fuel breaks and strategic guards all over the district. He had just finished four straight weeks of working on the night shifts and was happy to be once again working in the daylight.

By now forty minutes had passed since we had left the couple at their cottage. More and more clouds were beginning to take over the sky, so we decided to drive back up the road and check on the couple's progress. Approaching the cottage, we could see both of them on their hands and knees pulling weeds and digging through the soil in their front yard.

"What the…" Dash mumbled to himself while rolling his window down. "What are you doing, mate?" Dash said to the older gentleman.

"Just getting in some last minute gardening," he replied without looking away from his weeding.

"Get in your car. We are leaving," said Dash through a clenched jaw.

The couple stopped their weed pulling and looked up at us. "I thought you said we had an hour."

"Now!" Dash said as he rolled up his window. He then drove our Land Cruiser over to their vehicle to show them that we intended to leave. The couple brushed themselves off, got back into their station wagon, and followed us towards Alexandra.

"I guess they didn't understand the clear instructions we gave them," I said, trying not to laugh at the large vein that was bulging on Dash's forehead. Dash just muttered and cursed about how simpleminded some people could be.

Coming back through the blockade into Alexandra, I waved goodbye to the couple and continued on to the Depot. Arriving back in the yard, the sky had turned grey and was completely filled with ominous-looking clouds. I could feel the unfamiliar humidity building in the air that was coming from the incoming storm.

We filled in Kev about our morning and asked what he wanted us to do for the remainder of the day. "You guys can be done early, but only if you do one thing for me," Kev said. "Go to the pub and down a couple of beers; you've earned them." A wide smile spread across his face as we thanked him and let him know that was the best idea he had had in a long time.

We followed his orders and went straight to the pub. Some of the other firefighters who had received the same suggestion from Kev were already there. Nick, Dok, and Gretch had noticeably downed a few beers and greeted us with loud, happy greetings. Bonnie, Josh, and a Canadian buddy of mine also joined in our gathering as we unwound around our beer on the patio that overlooked the main street of Alexandra.

During the course of our gathering, the sky opened up and rewarded our efforts with the first drops of rain that we had felt in longer than I could remember. As the rain began to fall, disbelief turned into elation as everyone in the pub began to cheer and order more drinks. Each of us toasted the rain by clinking our beers and chugging whatever amount was left in our glasses. One by one, people left their seats and stood out in the rain. Some of the people, with their drinks still in their hands, went to the main intersection of town and danced as the rain fell around them. I joined the crowd in the streets and let the rain hit my face.

It was good to see my friends laugh and smile again, as it felt like it had been such a long time since any normality had been in our lives. The rain confirmed that the end was in sight and we could now release that sigh of relief that we had been holding in for far too long. No more wondering when the next person or house was going to be taken from us. No more working the long exhausting hours. No more uncertainty. It was finally over.

The following morning I decided that my tour of firefighting in Australia had come to an end. With the rain and cooler temperatures, the fires were under control and the rehabilitation phase of firefighting would begin. This entailed undoing all of the man-made damage such as reclaiming the dozer guards and fuel breaks that had been created throughout the forests. I wanted to spend the last four weeks I had in the country travelling and enjoying some much earned time off; besides, I wasn't overly fond of reclamation work anyways. The time off was also needed to rest and reset before I would start another fire season that was quickly approaching back in Canada. For over a month I had been fighting these fires, with only taking the minimum rest periods required by the job. I was physically, mentally, and emotionally spent. After everything that had transpired over the last 33 days since Black Saturday, I felt that I had done my part and fulfilled my work obligations.

Kev, Dave, and Hopper gave me permission to be done for the season. With smiles and handshakes they thanked me for my time of working for them and offered me a job the following fire season. Kev even had a look of sadness as he said his farewell to me. Of course, after working for the government there was lots of paperwork for me to fill out before I left. I returned all of my gear and emptied out my locker for the last time. The only piece of gear I didn't turn in was my green firefighting uniform. It felt strange not to have it with me, so I kept it as a keepsake.

Since it was Friday and the rain had halted the fires, most of the crew was in the Depot completing inventory checks or other off-line duties. I made a point of finding everyone that morning so I could invite them to a going away party that I was throwing the next day. I knew that some of the older blokes wouldn't be coming, so this was also my time to say some final goodbyes to people that I had come to bond with. I had developed a strong comradery with my workmates that could have only been formed out of the hardships we had faced together. It was difficult to come to a place so far away from home and develop friendships that would normally last a lifetime, and know that it might be the last time I would ever see these people who had become such a big part of who I was.

The going away party was not just an occasion for me to say goodbye to everyone that I had worked with over the three-and-a-half months; it was a time that everyone could use to unwind after what had happened. It was the first time all of us had hung out in a social setting since the fires had started and we could finally relax and enjoy the company of friends without having to wear our green uniforms.

That Saturday over 25 people showed up for the potluck dinner, with everyone bringing some sort of delicious food and drinks. After dinner was done but before we settled into party mode, Gogo got everyone's attention and asked me if I could join him in the middle of the backyard. He gave a quick speech about how this was my last day here and how much my work was appreciated. After a few jokes about how I wasn't that bad of a firefighter even though I was a Canadian, he shook my hand in gratitude and then presented me with a book called *Fire in the Rubicon*. Inside the cover of the book all of my co-workers and friends had written personal messages to me. I thanked the group as they gave me a round of applause. It was a very heartfelt moment that I still appreciate to this day.

Over the course of the night, more and more people arrived at my place to join in the festivities. Even some of the older office staff came out and let loose. With the aid of alcohol, I had several D & M's, as the Aussies say, or deep and meaningful conversations with the people I had become the closest to. It was emotional to say goodbye to my friends that I had come to care about. Gretch was by far the saddest to see me leave. I am happy I got the opportunity to get to know the Alexandra firefighters on such a personal level.

As the evening progressed and the party started to get out of hand, we moved to the Commercial pub and finished the remainder of the night there. Man those Aussies can drink.

I spent the next three weeks travelling up the Gold Coast in a camper van that Eben and another Canadian buddy of mine had rented. We did the typical tourist route and visited popular locations such as Sydney and its famous Opera House, Bondi Beach, and Surfers Paradise. We enjoyed the sun, attempted to surf, and had an enjoyable time. Once we arrived in Brisbane, I left my fellow Canadians and jumped on a plane back to Melbourne where I met up with Bonnie. From there, we caught a plane to Kuala Lumpur and spent a week relaxing on the beaches of the Tioman Islands located off of the east coast of Malaysia. It was a great way to end my trip before I returned home to Canada.

After five months of being overseas I was relieved to be back on Canadian soil. I got to skip the deep freeze of the Alberta winter and come back in the springtime when the forest was beginning to come back to life. I spent a week visiting with my friends and family before I left again to begin fighting fires for the SRD in Peace River.

Chapter 16

She'll be Right Mate

Black Saturday is a day that will always be remembered. Over 400 fires were reported to have started that afternoon which ultimately would burn over 450,000 hectares of land. Officially, 34 people lost their lives in Marysville and an additional 139 people died in adjacent areas for a total of 173 fatalities. 414 people were injured. 3,500 structures were burnt to the ground, displacing over 7,500 people from their homes.

The devastation that was brought upon the State of Victoria has forever left scars in the Australian people's hearts. But in the midst of all that loss there was hope, resilience, courage, and strength shown though the fellowship of the men and women who banded together to rebuild their communities. For some people the hardest part of the healing process was forgiving themselves. I too had a hard time letting go and the weight of my guilt felt heavy for years after that February seventh. For some unknown reason I felt as if I should have done more to protect the people that couldn't protect themselves.

Five years later, only a few weeks after my 30th birthday, I returned to Alexandra for another season as a wildland firefighter with the Department of Environment and Primary Industries formally known as the DSE. As much as I love being a firefighter, the reason for returning wasn't as simple as going just for the love of the job: I returned because the little voice in the back of my mind couldn't be ignored anymore and needed to be addressed. I needed to find some sort of closure to what had happened.

When I went back to Australia for the 2013/14 fire season I was once again accepted as one of their own. It felt as if I had never left. The majority of the same people were still working at the newly relocated, state of the art Depot that had been built in 2012 and would be used as a central command post if future large incidents occurred again in the area.

The excessive drought that was evident when I was there last had ended. With heavy winter rains in 2010 and average seasonal rainfall that followed, the drought was officially declared over. Lake Eildon that was once at 15% of its water holding capacity in 2009 is now up to 90%.

Five years had seen most of my friends get married and start families of their own. Being around them again further solidified the importance to me of the time I had spent there and how much it had altered my life. The changes were very positive in regards to the profession and the strides that they had taken to better themselves.

My good friend Pep now had five kids and was still happily married. He was still the same old Pep, just now a little wiser looking with grey highlights in his hair. He and I never talked about the Black Saturday fires, and I was told by a couple of the firefighters on base that he had never brought it up since that day.

Gogo was still the most passionate firefighter in both hemispheres.

I am grateful for the opportunities I had to work with the men and women of the Alexandra Depot. The bond of friendship that is created by firefighters who endure times of hardship does last a lifetime.

As expected, there were some major changes to the State in regards to how they fought and perceived bushfires. In February 2009, a Victorian Bushfires Royal Commission was conducted. With their findings, 67 recommendations were passed on to help ensure another tragedy would not occur. Some of these recommendations included a greater need for emergency evacuations and a higher level of communications between the DSE and the CFA. Nowhere in the Commission did it state that all fire personnel need radios on their persons at all times. If any of us had died, I would bet that would have been included. Residents could now be forced to evacuate if their homes are threatened by a bushfire, thus eradicating the "home is your castle" mentality. Very direct and intense commercials on television and radio explained the reality of bushfires and emphasized that leaving early is the key to survival.

Even after five years, the Black Saturday Bushfires was still a common topic for people to talk about or reference. It was still evident on a daily basis how much it had affected everyone and would continue to do so for years to come. During the five-year anniversary of February seventh, it was apparent that the memories were still fresh in the minds of those who had been impacted the most. These residents still talked about the fires as if they had just occurred the other day.

After two months of being back in Australia I finally mustered up the strength to return to Marysville. I wasn't sure what to expect or how I was going to feel, but it was something my heart knew I had to do.

Upon arrival, I was happy to see that the town that had once been almost completely destroyed was well on its way to being rebuilt. Some buildings were still under construction but it was a very different place from when I had seen it last. The first landmark I noticed was of a statue in a picture I had taken as I had left town that morning after Black Saturday. It was a bronze man with a child sitting on his shoulders looking through a pair of binoculars. Last time I saw this statue it had stood next to a white brick building that was badly damaged surrounded by burning trees. Now the statue was fashioned with a shiny red garland for the holiday season and a Victoria Bitters beer bottle placed in his outreached hand, as it stood alongside a newly constructed building.

From the statue I made my way up the hill and turned left onto Kings Road. Going further up the hill, the paved road turned into gravel and I continued to follow it for a couple hundred metres until I got to the corner of Martin Road. The hill was steeper than what I had remembered. The brown house that had once stood there was gone with a different house under construction in its place. The only evidence that a fire had ravaged this street was the black bark that still covered all the trees that remained. Each tree was now sheltered in leaves, hiding the evidence of what had happened that Saturday night. Looking over to the other side of the valley the scars of that fire still lingered. Entire hillsides remained void of old growth vegetation. Instead, thousands of large, grey toothpicks stood where there was once a great forest.

I walked to the exact spot where Josh and I had run for the burning truck and took a deep breath. I closed my eyes and silently thanked him for being so brave by jumping into a burning vehicle and bringing it to me. I looked at the new house under construction and knew for a fact that if it wasn't for Josh, the brown house that had once stood there would have been the last place I would have ever gone into. Thank you, Josh. I will forever be grateful to you for your heroism and for saving my life.

I walked over to the nearest tree and ripped off a piece of black bark that was still charred from that night. Then I placed it in my pocket.

I retraced my steps and drove my car to the reconstructed footie oval. Located on the corner of the field was Bruno's Art and Sculptures Garden. I went into the highly decorated shop and purchased a ticket to see his exhibit. After Bruno introduced himself to me, he immediately opened up a book at his front desk and showed me pictures of the Black Saturday bushfires. He talked about how much it had affected his life. He had lost hundreds of his paintings and sculptures.

Moving into the next room he showed off several pieces of art and explained how he was able to salvage some of it after the fires. At first I hadn't recognized him, but after a moment or two I realized that he was the artist that had been laying in his car that night. One painting on his wall was of a girl running from a burning hillside. There was a hole ripped through one side of the canvas. He explained that this was one of the paintings that he had saved before he was forced to flee from his house. He went on to explain that as he was getting into his car and about to drive to the oval, a black dog had run up to him. Wanting to save the whimpering dog, he had opened up the back door and let the dog jump in. While the dog was panicking in the back seat its leg had punched a hole through this painting. Bruno told me that he had added the fire to the hillside in the painting after that night.

It was uplifting to see that the residents of Marysville had decided to rebuild their town and carry on with their lives. I cannot speak for anyone else who was there, only myself, but I cannot imagine I am alone when I say that it is still difficult to think about that night. When I close my eyes I can still picture it as clear as if I am there. I have come to a point in my life where I have accepted what occurred and realized that I cannot change things that I had no control over. I am glad I had the opportunity to go back for a visit to Marysville and to see that even after something as terrifying and life changing as Black Saturday, people still have the courage to rebuild and move on.

We do our best to help safeguard our future. Only by learning from our mistakes can we ever truly move on and aid in our progression and understanding of one of nature's oldest destructive forces: fire.

CPSIA information can be obtained
at www.ICGtesting.com
Printed in the USA
BVOW09s0140230917
495620BV00003B/223/P